Successful
Dog Training

TS-205

Photographs by Corina Kamer unless otherwise noted.

Distributed in the UNITED STATES to the Pet Trade by T.F.H. Publications, Inc., One
T.F.H. Plaza, Neptune City, NJ 07753; distributed in the UNITED STATES to the
Bookstore and Library Trade by National Book Network, Inc. 4720 Boston Way, Lanham
MD 20706; in CANADA to the Pet Trade by H & L Pet Supplies Inc., 27 Kingston Crescent,
Kitchener, Ontario N2B 2T6; Rolf C. Hagen Ltd., 3225 Sartelon Street, Montreal 382
Quebec; in CANADA to the Book Trade by Macmillan of Canada (A Division of Canada
Publishing Corporation), 164 Commander Boulevard, Agincourt, Ontario M1S 3C7; in
ENGLAND by T.F.H. Publications, PO Box 15, Waterlooville PO7 6BQ; in AUSTRALIA
AND THE SOUTH PACIFIC by T.F.H. (Australia), Pty. Ltd., Box 149, Brookvale 2100
N.S.W., Australia; in NEW ZEALAND by Brooklands Aquarium Ltd. 5 McGiven Drive, New
Plymouth, RD1 New Zealand; in Japan by T.F.H. Publications, Japan—Jiro Tsuda, 10-12-
3 Ohjidai, Sakura, Chiba 285, Japan; in SOUTH AFRICA by Multipet Pty. Ltd., P.O. Box
35347, Northway, 4065, South Africa. Published by T.F.H. Publications, Inc.
MANUFACTURED IN THE UNITED STATES OF AMERICA
BY T.F.H. PUBLICATIONS, INC.

Successful
Dog Training

By Michael Kamer, Oblate, O.S.B.

Golden Retriever with his favorite training devices from Nylabone®: the Gumabone® and Nylabone® Frisbee®™. Photograph by Karen Taylor.

CONTENTS

The Praise Technique

All aspects of dog training for the accomplishment of obedience, responsiveness, nuisance problem elimination, and behavior modification which are discussed in this book are based on the Kamer Praise Technique. In my technique I maintain that praise, repetition, tone of voice, consistency and reasonable authority will enable you to train your dog in an enjoyable, loving manner.

We must accept that, by nature, dogs are pack animals and in the primal society whence they came, the pack was based on peer structure. Generally there would be one pack leader who would have achieved that position through the ability to be assertive and dominating over the balance of the pack. The pack would be submissive to this leader until such time that the leader exhibited discernible weakness. In the pack-type society living in the wilderness, puppies were free to dig, chew, jump, play fight and run. The same characteristics are present in the canine friends we choose to live with today.

Considering the fact that most of us live in domesticated and "civilized" societies, it falls upon us to educate our canine friends to acceptable limits so that they can fit into our urbanized lifestyles. Through praise, repetition, and tone of voice, we are able to achieve the desired domestication of our dogs without frustration and in a reasonably short period of time.

One of the main contentions of my technique is that puppies and dogs, much the same as children, have short attention spans when beginning training. This fact is the keystone to my praise technique. Typically speaking, when a dog commences training, this period of time will be 12 to 15 minutes. Whenever practicing any of the exercises taught in this book, train your dog within his attention span.

I recommend that you do this three to four times a day. The attention span will grow as training progresses. By training your dog in this manner, each session will be

An evening at home with Michael Kamer and graduate student "Monique."

interesting, energizing, and enjoyable to both of you. Your dog will look forward to seeing you come with its leash for each of the lessons because he will be anticipating a period of contact and learning with you. In addition, it has been my experience that most dogs wish to please and learn much the same as children. They're much happier when they understand their limits within the family structure.

Each training session shall begin with a short period of play which will be followed by the lesson. The lesson will always be concluded on an exercise that you know your dog knows well so that the lesson will always end on a positive note: namely, the ability to praise your dog for something he did well.

Introduction

The main thrust of this book is to teach your canine companion your language, your wishes, and the standards by which you wish him to live in relationship to you, your family and your home. However, I think it will be very rewarding to take a moment to consider the language used by dogs. Dogs will use not only facial expressions, eye expressions, or mouth expressions but also body language and tail language to relate what they are thinking, what they want, and how they feel. When a dog communicates through utilization of his voice, he will use a number of different sounds: for example, deep, thrusting barks in a husky manner normally mean that something is strange or odd or that the puppy is feeling threatened in the area. By the same token, high, sharp yips or cries say that something is wrong or that the puppy is in trouble. Short yippie-type barks accompanied by prancing around and wagging his tail will generally mean that the puppy wishes attention or wants to play. A mournful howl usually relates that the puppy is lonely, wants companionship, or misses you. A growl, on the other hand, generally says don't bother me, stay away, or, once again, something is wrong. Next consider ears—usually when your dog's ears are alert, he is listening to something that seems odd or peculiar to him. Ears down usually

"Elijah," our Old English Mastiff.

Michael Kamer poses with a favorite student.

means that the puppy is relaxed or something might be frightening him. For me personally, eye expression carries with it the most dramatic doggie communication. My wife Corina has an Old English Mastiff named "Elijah," and we find his eyes to be extremely expressive. Through eyes and facial expression alone, we can tell when he wishes to go out, when someone may be outside the door, when he wants to play, or when he simply wants to be left alone to take a nap. Tails are much the same as flags to a dog: when the tail is up and wagging, your dog is generally going to be happy and excited; when his tail is down, he is either relaxed or calm; when his tail is tucked up underneath his body, this generally indicates fear. Although we have discussed voice, eyes and tail, I think you will find that if you spend any degree of quality time with your dog, you will see that each dog tends to have a unique way of relating to his human master what he thinks, what he desires, and how he feels. Once you have lived with your dog for a period of time and have spent time observing his "language," you will find it much easier not only to live with him but also to train him. I, for example, over the years have learned to predict pretty accurately how the puppy student is going to respond: bolt, be stubborn, or act shy or perplexed. For me, this is normally transmitted by body language and facial expression. As you develop your relationship with your dog and learn to interpret your dog's body language and facial expressions, you will find they will assist you in not only training him but understanding his moods and being able to respond in an appropriate manner to each.

Over a period of months and years, I have found with all the dogs that I have owned that, in addition to the formal training we will be discussing in the book, it is very important to develop a personal language between yourself and your dog. The areas we have thus covered are nuances into a closer and more intimate relationship with your dog. You and your dog will develop what I refer to as pseudo-commands, which become rather exclusive to only you and your dog. Such things as "Do you want a treat?, Where's your ball?, Do you want to go for a walk?, Where's mom?," and so on. All these become part of your dog's vocabulary and extend your ability to communicate with him. Many times I find myself actually talking to my dog—I don't profess that he understands each and every word of what I'm saying, but I do believe the projected overtone of what I'm saying is understood by my dog. Dogs perceive sadness, happiness, loneliness, anger, and fear, and respond in many ways the same as we human beings would. I think this nature of a dog is probably what makes him the most profound companion of mankind bar none. The ability to interpret his master's gestures, moods, tones of voice, and needs makes it possible for the dog to succeed to a degree of intimacy with humankind exceeded by no other animal. Consider for a moment the amount of love, affection, reward, protection, companionship, and loyalty that a dog gives for nothing more than a pat on the head, a word of praise here and there, a place to sleep, and a share of food. I think we human beings would be well advised to take a most profound lesson from these characteristics.

Dogs have accompanied man throughout history, migrations and immigrations, and have gone faithfully to all points of the earth, responding as needed to whatever task

The dog is not only willing but eager to fulfill the needs of his master and be content with whatever role within the family structure he is given.

I have also found in my career that a dog will respond to his master

Michael Kamer and student "Murphy," a three-month-old female Mastiff.

put at hand with zeal and loyalty. In this crazy, mixed-up world in which we find ourselves living, with its fickle value systems and ethics, I think it is astounding to find that, regardless of country, race or religion of the people, wealth or poverty of the country, the very same attributes that have devoted the dog to mankind are still found.

much like a child does to his parents. In a family where I am asked to work with a very unruly, undisciplined dog, I will generally find that the children's relationship with the parents is about on the same level. Then again, in a family where I find that the children are well supervised and reasonable authority is present so that the children have healthy limits, the training and adapting of a new dog to the family require a minimal effort.

I think this is very important to consider when you are adding a new member to the family and thus a new catalyst. It's important to consider not only what breed, what size, what temperament of dog you're going to look for but, how equipped the family is as a whole to deal with a new puppy. I would venture to say that selection of a new dog based on temperament and intelligence by far supersedes selection of a dog by breed, size, or color. And so, in considering the dog for your family, I would make a strong recommendation to investigate the overviews of personalities in the prospective breeds that you are considering. Some breeds of dog, because they were bred specifically for particular tasks initially, do carry certain traits. For example, hunting dogs tend to be rather dogmatic, while dogs that were bred for rodent killing such as the terriers can be very stubborn and pugnacious. Whereas these particular characteristics were desired for the tasks of these dogs in years of old,

they may not be suitable for the overall disposition, temperament, or tenor of your particular family. When you are selecting your puppy based on the family's desire for a particular dog, consider overall temperament and pace of the family and look for a breed similarly inclined. For example, a family that likes to spend a lot of time relaxing, reading and doing other sedentary activities would be well advised to pick a dog with a similar temperament. Needless to say, selecting a capricious playful dog, such as a West Highland White Terrier, might tip the teakettle, so to speak, and create a problem within the family. By the same token, if you have a family that is very energetic and active and/or there are youngsters in the family that enjoy playing and romping, you would be well advised to pick a dog of the same temperament. There are many excellent dog encyclopedias and breed standard books on the market in which you can preview the different breeds that you are interested in. The best of them is *The Atlas of Dog Breeds of the World*, published by T.F.H. Publications, Inc. I highly recommend this book as a tool by which you can familiarize yourself not only with the many breeds and/or within the family structure. When a dog is growing up within a family, he is like a little computer

Leandra Kamer and student friend "Murphy."

available but also with the temperament, size, and inclinations of each particular breed. Then compare this portrait to the lifestyle, needs, and desires of your family. This process will help preclude the many travesties I have seen when people have bought new dogs on impulse.

The nature of the typical dog is very malleable in that the dog can become whatever the family wills or allows it to become within the relationship with its human owners turned on constantly intaking information. If the environment and framework of the family structure are conducive to growth, you will find developing in the puppy a nature by which he is responding directly to this environment and in fact taking advantage. Not necessarily that the puppy willed to do this, but rather that, by the lack of appropriate or more directed supervision, the puppy's natural instincts and propensities begin to take over. By the same token, one can have a specific breed such as a German Shepherd or an Australian Shepherd or a Cocker Spaniel within a family and the encouragement of the family in a positive direction will be taken in by the puppy who becomes very responsive and very heedful of the parameters that the family has preset. In addition, encouragement in such areas being naturally protective or development in becoming a "lap dog" can come about naturally by the attitude of the family toward the dog. For example, if you would tend to praise a puppy who has just barked because he or she heard a noise outside the house, which the family deems an appropriate noise to be responded to, you will find very quickly that your puppy, enjoying such praise, will begin to bark naturally at those types of noises. By the same token, if you wished to have a dog within the family that was more apt to overlook a great deal of miscellaneous noises outside the house rather than a dog that will respond to specific noises, a correction of "No! No!" to a young puppy could abort a developing problem in the young adult.

Another example might be the person who enjoys having a dog sit with him for hours very benignly, simply for companionship. Most young dogs enjoy being petted and stroked and having quality time spent with them. This can become a rather rewarding personal area of your relationship with your dog if properly encouraged. However, you would quite quickly find tiring or tedious a puppy that is constantly licking or who is constantly wanting attention. In fact, over a period of months and years, this could develop into a puppy who becomes quite demanding and a nuisance.

Dogs pick up very quickly on the tempo and nature of the family as well. For example, if you and your family are hikers, your young puppy will very quickly, if taken along, grow to enjoy these walks and look forward to them. I think we've all heard stories about the individual who had a dog that went to the closet where the leash was kept, anticipating going out for his walk. Well, the same thing takes place when we have varying activities that we do on a regular basis with our dogs. Dogs imprint on these activities as well as on the gear related to it. I have a client who rides her horses quite regularly and takes her dog with her to the barn. She has found that whenever she reaches for riding boots, her dog becomes quite excited and happy and runs to the front door. The dog knows that the donning of the boots means that mom is going to the barn, and she is looking forward to the ride on the trail, with the horse, with whom she has become quite friendly, as well as with her owner. Dogs have very competent memories, and can relate to instances of enjoyment, such as mom's going for her riding boots or the master's preparing for the hike.

Dogs not only relate to positive experiences and store them in their memories but also remember incidences which cause fear or unhappiness. I think many times we also underestimate the ability of dogs to evaluate situations. I'd like to cover these issues one at a time. I have found—and you will too—that when a dog experiences certain procedures on a regular

"Bismark" is a three-month-old Rottweiler student.

basis they become habitual. Dogs are as much a product of habit as are we; when breakfast is fed at a certain time, walks are conducted at a certain time, and play periods or lessons are held at a certain time, your dog, having a built-in natural clock, can sense these times. The dog will begin to display physical nuances which, if read appropriately by a family member or by his owner, indicate that the dog is aware of what is about to occur.

Dogs also remember places. Once or twice a year my family and I go to a mountain cabin for skiing and recreation, and we have found over the several years that we have gone that our dog remembers the cabin and the area quite well. The varying attitudes of our dog indicate to us that he remembers certain aspects of a trail or places in the town, and most assuredly his spot in the cabin.

Dogs have a great deal more evaluative capability than I think most people realize. I'll relate the following instance: one year when we were up at the cabin, a particular trail that we usually hike on had been barricaded by some fallen trees. Our dog,

proceeding ahead of us, became aware of this particular problem. He seemed quite puzzled as to how he was going to continue the trek. We elected to hang back a bit without his realizing that we were observing how he would deal with this unexpected obstacle. He first went to one side of the road, which was a steep embankment, and realizing that this was too much of an embankment for him to deal with, retreated posthaste from that position. He then went to the other side of the road, which was a bit of a hill but not nearly as steep an embankment, and proceeded around the fallen trees, stopped abruptly, backed up, gave a wide berth to a particular area of level snow, went around that area, and came back down onto the road on the far side of the trees. When my wife and I approached the area, we were puzzled by the fact that he wouldn't cross this apparently level packed snow. I took a branch from one of the fallen trees and poked it down into the ground to find that it was quite deep, and that below it was frozen water. I think this clearly indicates the dog's perception or ability to analyze a situation quite readily.

Another time I was training a dog for an individual at a park where the owner had told me the dog had been several times. After the lesson, we walked over to a refreshment stand which the owner apparently frequented, but it was apparently closed. When the dog heard his master say, "I guess they're closed," the dog walked around to the back of the stand and then ran back to us wagging his tail, barking as if we should follow. Around the back of the stand, we found that the owner was still in the refreshment stand and the back door was open, and we were able to obtain our drinks. I think this clearly indicates that dogs have the ability to learn knowledge, and not only to learn it but to store it and draw upon it at a later instance to deal with a given situation.

Dogs also have probably the most loyal devotion to their owners that I have ever experienced among human or animal. I don't really think a dog would think twice about laying down his life for the safety of his master. One year I was out at the beach and had brought a large

inflatable tube from a tire; I proceeded to go out into the ocean in the tube, made myself comfortable, and with the soft lull of the ocean fell asleep. In the far distance, after a while, I heard my dog barking. I opened my eyes to see that I had been pulled out by an undertow quite far from the shore. Looking back at the shore, I saw my dog swimming out toward me. I'm quite sure "Sheba," this particular dog who is no longer with us, had

Trainer Francisco Gomez and student "Boda," a German Shepherd at seven months.

evaluated that this was a very dangerous situation for me and had leaped in posthaste to do whatever she could do to help me.

Another instance I recall occurred many, many years ago when I was in the United States Air Force. I was walking a distant perimeter post after a very large snowstorm, and approached an area that my dog was reluctant to pass by. I, "knowing better than the dog," proceeded and fell through snow and ice into water. The dog promptly lay down, making himself an anchor, which enabled me to pull myself to the side, and eventually up and out of this hole by the dog's leash. The dog had not been formerly taught to do this in this type of situation, but I was certainly glad that he responded in the way that he did.

The companionship, the natural loyalty and the selflessness that I have found in their devotion to man are unmatched by any other animal that I have seen. I think we human beings would do well to take this fine example of a dog's nature with his family.

Many times when I'm ruminating about my experiences with dogs, I think to myself how stable, faithful and obedient our dogs are. They are not generally greedy; they don't really care whether they have a large area or a small area to live; they are not the most particular eaters; they tend to not complain very much if their owner's schedule is quite busy and they don't get the same amount of time they're used to getting. They are patient beyond reason; they are loyal to a fault; and their natural proclivity towards membership in a family could be well taken by most of us humans today. I've heard many people say, "I much prefer the companionship of my dog to that of human people; they're predictable, trustworthy, loyal, and they can be depended upon." I think we are very fortunate in our relationship with our dogs to have such a marvelous being elected to be our companion and partner.

Dogs have been used for varying tasks, from the sublime to the ridiculous— from dressing them up as clowns in a circus to search dogs locating and helping to recover lost children in the woods and lost travellers in the Alpine snow. Their capability in adapting to climatic

changes as well as living conditions of the family is extraordinary. Dogs have been taught to coach fire wagons drawn by horses; dogs have been taught to hunt, to retrieve, to alert, to search, to detect; dogs have been taught to carry messages through bombblast and gunfire. Dogs have been taught to draw wagons; dogs have been taught to cohabit with just about all other kinds of animals. Dogs adapt themselves, and learn to make do with whatever their human master elects to provide them and consider it ample. As long as a dog is given a little bit of food and a pat on the head, and his human master loves and cares for him, a dog is satisfied and content.

I was privileged to hear a story about an elderly man who had had a dog for many years, and lived in a small town in Massachusetts by the air base at which I was stationed. After the elderly man passed away, the dog was given to family relatives. However, each day the dog would leave these people's yard and would be found at its master's gravesite, several miles from the home and town. Dogs have a very strong sense of direction. Many times I have gone

Siberian Husky "Max", a nine-month-old male student on a long off-leash "Down" command.

hiking and have found myself lost, and have turned to my dog and said, "Okay, T.J., it's up to you." T.J. has picked up this cue, started using his nose and ultimately led us back to a main trail or area from which I was able to help finish our return.

Once upon a time I was snorkeling off the coast of Catalina, which is a small island off the coast of California, and had taken my German Shepherd Dog with me. In the course of snorkeling, I had been so enthralled by what I was watching below that I failed to realize that a current was pulling me down the length of the island. After a while I looked up and realized I had gone quite a distance from where I had started and saw my dog nowhere in sight. Swimming perpendicular to the current, I finally got ashore some five miles from where I had left our jeep. As I sat on the sand catching my breath and pondering the return trip, over a knoll soaked and tired came the panting Sheba who had followed me all of those miles. Actually, all along the shoreline at various points, she was required to jump into the ocean to swim around a pier and other obstacles. She was

dogmatically attuned to the fact that where I went she was going as well, and followed me until she was able to get to my side. Needless to say, I was greeted by a big wet kiss and a big wet dog, and I don't remember when I was so glad to see her.

Dogs can be taught to do just about anything. In my career as a dog trainer, I have trained dogs to work in the movies, to walk up ladders, to walk tightropes, to push carts, to pull carts, to wave flags, to ride surfboards, to ride a tricycle, and to wear clothes. I can't think of anything that, given enough patience and time, a socialized, family-oriented dog cannot be taught to do.

Patience and love are the two most important elements in any relationship with a dog, and I might say with people as well. Dogs are extremely patient, when you realize the abuse that small children unknowingly levy on most family pets. It's a wonder the dog survives; however, he does seem to know that this is a child and that he is to be tolerant. Regardless of whether it's putting his ears in a bow, dressing him up in clothes and putting him in a carriage, or making the most unreasonable demands of him, the dog is extremely patient and tolerant of children as a whole and even when only moderately neglected, such as when his owner is extremely busy and doesn't have the quality that of a sergeant who had found a small stray puppy. Through the campaign, he carried the puppy inside of his vest. I think most major television stations carried the story, and there were scenes of the puppy sleeping on his master's chest on a break,

time that one would normally like to spend each day with his dog. Dogs are very patient, and will adjust to and accept that, at this point in time, they can't necessarily have exactly what they would want.

It's interesting to note that in the Iraqi war one of the well-noted stories was his head peering out of the sergeant's bullet-proof vest while on patrol. I think this epitomizes the extent to which a dog will acclimate himself and accept an unusual pattern for daily life so that he could be with his human master.

We note that most emperors, kings, queens,

Leandra Kamer and friend "Murphy."

presidents and many heads of states are all associated with dogs and some are dog fanciers of a specific breed. The dogs have been recorded in our history since man first learned to draw on the wall of a cave, memorialized throughout the ages in paintings, sculptures, jewelry, poetry, and literature. Despite the differences that mankind has had throughout the history of time—different nations, different governments, different races, different religions—men share a common affection for the dog and afford it an important place within the social structure. From the mastiffs of Europe to the Pharaoh hounds of Egypt to the dingo of the Aborigines, men have somehow chosen the dog as their companion. Even in devastation and hard times, the dog has always been so revered as companion, protector, and community member that any time a people has found it necessary to migrate—be it the American Indians, the Polynesians, the Tahitians, the Eskimos or any major movement of people as in the crusades or the world wars, dogs can always be found among the refugees. I hope this gives you, the student and reader, some insight into what your dog brings to your family. This is why it's so all-important to make sure that you are properly prepared for this new family member, and are cognizant of the fact that your dog means you well, would love to fit into your family appropriately, and needs you to teach him the necessary mores of living within your family structure. Given the time and the opportunity as well as the training to properly adjust, associate and relate to his new home, your dog and you will enter into a relationship that can be the most fulfilling, loving and rewarding one that anyone ever experienced on this earth.

Acquiring Your Dog

When you are ready to purchase your dog, I strongly recommend staying away from backyard breeders. These are people who mean well, but generally know very little about the line they are breeding. The story might be: Jim had one, and Mary had one, and they were friends. They thought it would be really neat to have puppies and so they bred their dogs. This type of breeding, although it may be a lot of fun for the people doing it, can many times result in poor-quality dogs. It is very necessary to consider the strong and weak points of both the male and female of a breeding, prior to the actual mating. In addition, pedigrees should be examined to prevent breeding into a line that might carry hereditary or congenital illnesses. I also recommend staying away from what are known as puppymills. These are generally people that have a number of female dogs of various breeds and breed primarily for quantity as opposed to quality. I suggest trying to locate a breeder in your area that is a serious hobbyist; someone preferably that has some other type of full-time profession, but breeds dogs as a serious hobby. Many times you will find these same people are dog-show exhibitors. They will generally breed one or two litters a year. The litters are raised in their homes, not outside somewhere in an austere kennel, but rather the puppies are an integral part of the family. Thus, you are purchasing not only a puppy who is bred with discretion but also one who has already been socialized to living in the human family environment. This alone can save you many hours of aggravation, and many unnecessarily spent dollars at the veterinarian, as well as gross disappointments. Always deal with a breeder who is deeply concerned about where the puppy will be living, what type of family environment the puppy will be exposed to, and how much time you will have to give the puppy. Although some breeders who are overly concerned seem to be unnecessarily zealous about the placement of their puppies, I think this clearly denotes someone who takes a great deal of care, concern and pride in his puppies and their potential homes, much the same as you would if you were going to be leaving your child at a school or camp. Always deal with a breeder who not only allows but requests that you have the puppy given a complete physical by your veterinarian within 48 hours of purchase. These types of breeders generally take deep concern that you know the puppy is healthy and want your independent veterinarian to confirm what they are saying. These types of breeders will generally give you a cash-back guarantee if the veterinarian should find anything seriously wrong. Many reputable breeders these days will also guarantee that the dog is free of congenital and hereditary illnesses. I strongly recommend dealing with breeders like this who generally take a great deal of care to preclude any type of undesirable propensity that could manifest itself within that particular breed. Many breeds do carry genes for certain hereditary or congenital illnesses. Breeders of such dogs, who take care and pride in their litters, will go out of their way to make sure that they have done everything possible to preclude their puppies carrying or passing on those genes.

Whenever I am selecting a puppy for a client of ours, I always select the dog from a reputable quality breeder. I then evaluate the dog for temperament, intelligence, and trainability. I then take the puppy to our veterinarian for a complete physical, from nose to tail, with the full understanding that the puppy can be returned if the veterinarian determines anything serious. Once a person has obtained the new puppy, he generally tends to bond with and become loyal to the new family member very quickly. For this reason, if for no other, I strongly recommend taking the precautions that I describe. I cannot begin to tell you how many times I have seen people buy poor-quality puppies on an impulse from people who breed inappropriately; these puppies have exhibited problems such as hyperactivity, mental sluggishness, and general bad health. Occasionally, I have also had to evaluate puppies for training that had hereditary or congenital illnesses. It would seem a very sad state of affairs to have fallen in love with a new puppy only to find that, for the rest of that puppy's life, it would have to be on some type of treatment or medication. By following the procedures described here, you should avoid becoming victimized by these types of problems.

Now that you have selected your new puppy and have brought him home, let's get him off to a good start with the family. It is very important that the puppy have an area of his own. Depending upon the time of year and climate, this area may be indoors or out, but it should have certain commonalities. The area should be puppy-safe, meaning that the puppy cannot get out of the area or get into anything dangerous. In addition, you certainly want to remove anything from the area that could be destroyed inadvertently or that could be a danger to the puppy. The puppy should have a dry, room-temperature area in which to sleep. Whether this be a dog house, the utility room, or an area of your garage, it should be equipped with the amenities of necessity for a young dog. I recommend a few safe chew toys (likely your puppy has bonded with its Nylabone® or Gumabone®), some appropriate bedding, and, if need be, a wind-up clock. I find that the ticking of a clock to a puppy many times equates with that of the heartbeat of his mother, and may minimize a lot of unnecessary whining or

Another Kamer student, "Buddha" is a three-month-old male Japanese Akita.

crying when it's time for puppy to go to sleep. Make sure as you integrate puppy to the family that it gets a great deal of quality time with all members of the family, adults and children, in a safe, reasonable manner. Do not allow young children to be excessively demonstrative, boisterous, or rough with the new puppy. Not only could the puppy be hurt but the puppy might become afraid of loud children. Children should be instructed to appreciate that this is a baby and should be treated as gently and kindly as we would a human baby. It is wise to continue the same diet that the breeder recommends, because most breeders take a great deal of care and time to research quality foods that work well with their breed and line. So, unless your veterinarian suggests otherwise, you will generally find that your breeders have made an excellent choice for your puppy. Puppy's feeding schedule should be regulated as you would a human child's. Most young puppies eat three times a day. I recommend these times be the first thing in the morning, around noon, and three or four in the afternoon. The reason I

recommend this time for the last meal is so that puppy has plenty of time to digest and evacuate this meal, and, when puppy is put to bed in his safe clean quarters, he won't find himself in a situation where he has to eliminate in his bed. All housebreaking and similar puppy training procedures should be well in place before formal obedience training begins. This way we know we have taken care of puppy's necessities and that the puppy has become well adapted and acclimated to his new home. Periods of time should be spent acclimating the puppy to his new home. The puppy should be contained one way or another as you spend quality time with him. Some of this time may be spent in exercise and play but there should also be some quality time spent simply relaxing, such as if you were watching television or sitting and reading.

The methods of containment in this type of situation can be a collar and a leash, so that, if puppy starts to get up and go some place he shouldn't, you can easily contain him. If puppy should indicate by body language and gesture that he needs to go potty, he can quickly be picked up in your arms and taken to the appropriate area.

SELECTING A DOG

Selection of both the best dog for training and for breeding can be made through aptitude tests. The following is a brief overview of aptitude tests that I use to determine the personality and trainability of a puppy. Place the puppy in an open area and allow him to get engrossed in playing a bit. Walk away, clap your hands, and coax the puppy to you to determine the degree of the puppy's social ability. Generally we're looking for a puppy that will readily come with his tail up and wagging. Following this, walk about with the puppy, talking to him. See if the puppy follows you. Another thing to look for is the ability to pick a puppy up, turn him on his back, and hold him in your arms while you pet his tummy. A secure, calm puppy will allow you to do this readily, while an insecure, nervous or hyper puppy will not. The puppy's intelligence can be gauged by playing with a little squeaky toy or ball that the puppy enjoys. Toss it to see if he will run after it, is curious and picks it up and brings it back to you. All of these are very positive

signs and show a puppy of good intelligence. To determine the pup's confidence, place him in an area, walk away, and make a sudden loud noise such as clanging keys. We want a puppy that will calmly look up to try to determine where the noise is coming from or what it's about. Generally puppies that are sensitive or lack self-confidence will get scared by the loud noise, possibly even run away, shake or tremble.

Three-year-old male Australian Cattle Dog "T.J."

Elements for Training

TONE OF VOICE

In training your dog, tone of voice is exceedingly important. Our technique utilizes three distinctly different tones of voice: The praising tone of voice, which will be a higher tone of voice to say such things as "Good dog! Good dog! That's the way! What a Good dog!"; the commanding tone of voice, which will be a monotone to say "Come, Sit, Stay, Down"; and the reprimanding tone of voice, which will be a dropping of the voice (i.e., imagine yourself diving off of a diving board) to say "Baad Doog, Noo!"— the voice lowers from the beginning to the end of the word. Excessive volume is not necessary with any of these tones, but rather what is preferred is a normal conversational tone of voice. We want your dog to learn to respond to you in a civilized manner, without your having to use excessive volume or shouting. You will find that your dog will quickly become accustomed to your applications of the appropriate tones of voice: namely, praise indicated by raising the voice;

commands in a steady monotone; reprimands by the deep dropping of the voice. You will have good communication and appropriate control of your dog with a minimal amount of effort by using these guidelines.

Dogs respond as much to your body language as they do to your verbal commands and hand signals. Practice in busy environments so your dog will become acclimated to working with distractions. Don't allow the dog to control the lesson, i.e., to stop when he wants, to sit when he wants, etc. The dog may do this naively in the beginning but soon will learn that he can control the lesson.

USE OF HAND SIGNALS

Our technique makes extensive use of hand signals as well as voice commands. Initially in training, each time we teach the dog a new exercise, it will be done through a combination of voice command and hand signal. The hand signal is a physical motion that assists you in guiding the dog into the proper position through contact of

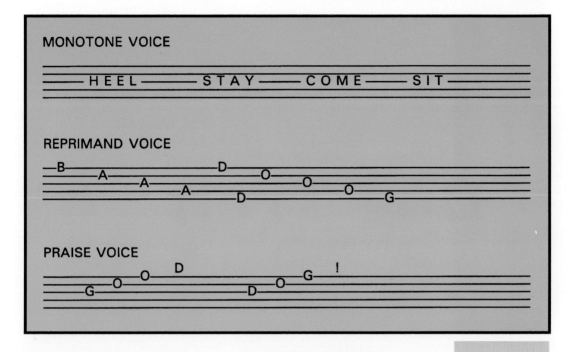

MONOTONE VOICE

HEEL — STAY — COME — SIT

REPRIMAND VOICE

B — A — A — A — D — D — O — O — O — G

PRAISE VOICE

G — O — O — D — D — O — G — !

the hand with the dog's body. When your dog sees, hears, and feels "the lesson," he will learn much more quickly. You are literally exposing three of his senses to the learning process. Each hand signal that will be used at first should be given dramatically in a large way, so that your dog will become accustomed to the various gestures and their corresponding instructions.

As training progresses and your dog becomes more efficiently trained, the hand signals can become more subtle. You will find, when your dog is efficiently trained, the slightest nuance of a hand signal from his master will evoke the desired response. In addition, you will find once your dog has completed training, he will respond to either voice commands or hand signals, as well as the combination thereof.

You will find that there are times when a voice command may be more appropriate than a hand signal, or vice versa. For example, if you are occupied on the telephone or talking to someone and you want your dog to sit, lay down or stay, it would be much less inconvenient to simply give the dog the hand signal as opposed to interrupting your conversation to address your dog. Likewise, if your dog was turned away from you or was some distance from you and you wished your dog to come, it would be more effective to use a voice command as opposed to a hand signal. Initially, however, hand signals should be used in conjunction with voice commands.

DESCRIPTION OF HAND SIGNALS

The hand signal for "STAY" is an extending of the right hand outward, much the same way a policeman would to stop traffic. So you say "Stay" to your dog and extend the hand outwardly. When your dog is sitting at your left side in the "Heel" position, "Stay" would be given with the left hand simply being released from the leash and dropped down about two feet in front of the dog's nose. You will notice it is more convenient to use the left hand in this instance than it would be to put the leash into your left hand so that your right hand can come across in front of you and give the dog the hand signal.

The hand signal for "COME" is a beckoning motion toward your chest with your right hand, much the same as you would call to a friend across the street.

The hand signal for "DOWN" is a downward motion of the right index finger starting above your head and swinging down briskly toward the ground.

The hand signal for "STAND" is an upward wiggling of the fingers.

The hand signal for "FINISH" is a tapping on the right hip, the hand signal for heeling would be a tapping of the left hip.

The hand signal for "SIT" is a quick upward motion of the right forearm, with the hand open and the palm facing the sky.

TRAINING TIPS

Lots of practice with handling your dog correctly and application of the training methods in real-life situations are the prerequisite to control during times of excitement as well as the means of building a bond between your dog and you.

What we don't want is a conditioned response where a dog learns his commands in a particular routine. A true creature of habit, he will know his commands only in routine. We want him to understand each command individually. Most people tend to rush. That's not good because they literally condition the dogs to not be patient in holding any of their positions. So I would rather see you count to 20 or 30 between commands so he gets the idea.

A dog must have some play every day even during the period you are training with him, but he should never be allowed to contract bad habits which will have to be eliminated later on. For example, if he tugs at your clothes tell him "No, bad dog." Some people have said to me, "Oh, I like my dog to act naturally." My feeling is that you can have a natural dog who enjoys all the natural things in life and still has respect and obedience for his family.

COLLAR AND LEASH

Prior to beginning heeling exercises or any other training procedures

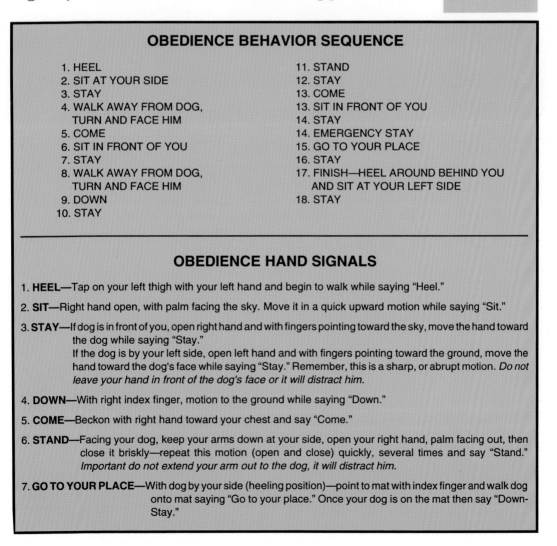

OBEDIENCE BEHAVIOR SEQUENCE

1. HEEL
2. SIT AT YOUR SIDE
3. STAY
4. WALK AWAY FROM DOG, TURN AND FACE HIM
5. COME
6. SIT IN FRONT OF YOU
7. STAY
8. WALK AWAY FROM DOG, TURN AND FACE HIM
9. DOWN
10. STAY
11. STAND
12. STAY
13. COME
13. SIT IN FRONT OF YOU
14. STAY
14. EMERGENCY STAY
15. GO TO YOUR PLACE
16. STAY
17. FINISH—HEEL AROUND BEHIND YOU AND SIT AT YOUR LEFT SIDE
18. STAY

OBEDIENCE HAND SIGNALS

1. **HEEL**—Tap on your left thigh with your left hand and begin to walk while saying "Heel."

2. **SIT**—Right hand open, with palm facing the sky. Move it in a quick upward motion while saying "Sit."

3. **STAY**—If dog is in front of you, open right hand and with fingers pointing toward the sky, move the hand toward the dog while saying "Stay."
   If the dog is by your left side, open left hand and with fingers pointing toward the ground, move the hand toward the dog's face while saying "Stay." Remember, this is a sharp, or abrupt motion. *Do not leave your hand in front of the dog's face or it will distract him.*

4. **DOWN**—With right index finger, motion to the ground while saying "Down."

5. **COME**—Beckon with right hand toward your chest and say "Come."

6. **STAND**—Facing your dog, keep your arms down at your side, open your right hand, palm facing out, then close it briskly—repeat this motion (open and close) quickly, several times and say "Stand." *Important do not extend your arm out to the dog, it will distract him.*

7. **GO TO YOUR PLACE**—With dog by your side (heeling position)—point to mat with index finger and walk dog onto mat saying "Go to your place." Once your dog is on the mat then say "Down-Stay."

with your new puppy, I recommend that you acclimate the puppy to wearing both a collar and leash in the following manner.

When you first get your puppy, place a light-weight rolled leather or nylon collar on your puppy. Make sure that you get one that's easily adjustable. Your puppy will be growing considerably in the first year of his life, so we want to make sure that you can easily adjust the collar as it becomes necessary. If your puppy will accept wearing a collar, allow the puppy to wear a collar whenever the puppy can be under supervision. If you need to leave the puppy alone, always make sure to remove the collar so that there's no chance of the puppy getting tangled in or caught on the collar.

If you see that your puppy does not like wearing a collar, but rather scratches at it, tries to rub it off on the ground or on walls, and is constantly annoyed by its presence, you'll have to approach this training more slowly. Start off by having the puppy wear the collar for brief periods of time, to exceed no more than 10 or 15 minutes. Put the collar on the puppy two or three times a day until it becomes apparent that the puppy accepts the collar. Then, increase the time that you allow the puppy to wear the collar to a half hour, and then to an hour. Once again this should be done over a period of days and weeks—do not try to accomplish this goal in a matter of hours. Once it is apparent that the puppy will allow the collar to stay on, leave it on all of the time when he is supervised so that he will be accustomed to wearing it.

CHAIN LEASH

Now that your puppy has learned to accept wearing a collar easily, and permits it on for hours on end, we'll add a lightweight, short chain leash. This should be hooked to the "D" ring on your puppy's collar. Your puppy should be allowed to drag this around with him for short periods, starting with 15 minutes. We are building up to a point where your puppy will become comfortable dragging this short chain leash around for a matter of an hour or two at a time. The purpose of this is to preclude the puppy's balking when you first start walking with him on a leash in the heeling exercise. We have found this works quite well. Once again, this should only be done when there will be a period of time that you can keep your puppy in constant observance. We don't want to leave an unattended or unsupervised puppy alone with a collar and leash on for obvious reasons. The puppy could snag this leash or collar on some item and panic or he could snag it on something and hurt himself. You must always be right there to help. If you notice that your puppy tends to fight with the chain leash, allow this as long as the response is playful and the puppy is not too upset. If for any reason it seems to upset your puppy terribly, comfort the puppy and try to convince him to allow this on for short periods of time. Generally speaking, most puppies do not mind carrying

around the short chain leash and will sometimes play with it. Rarely have I come upon dogs who are upset by the leash. They require a gentler hand as well as shorter beginning times of no more than five minutes of pulling the chain around. Be sure the pup is thoroughly acclimated to the leash before commencing formal heeling exercises.

The No-Pull Halter provides maximum control without choking your dog.

Using the Praise Technique

"HEEL"

Heeling is the canine discipline of walking parallel to your left side, following at every turn; stopping automatically each time you stop; and sitting automatically when you come to a halt. The purpose of this practice is to accommodate both you and your dog on daily walks as well as in public or congested situations.

The tools for this lesson will be a six-foot leather training leash approximately one inch wide and a slip chain of an appropriate length to your dog's neck. For example: a 24-inch slip chain would be used for a typical German Shepherd, and 18 inches for a smaller dog and so on. There should be

Proper manner of placing a slip chain on your dog's neck.

approximately two inches of slip chain between the loose link and the leash, when the slip chain is pulled comfortably snug on your dog's neck. This will enable you to release the slip chain as well as to snap it when it becomes necessary.

Heeling is taught in the following way. Place your slip chain on your dog so that the loop that is connected to the leash is coming over your dog's left shoulder toward you and the loose link is resting on your dog's right shoulder. If the slip chain is on correctly, when you pull up, the slip chain will be snug on your dog's neck. When you release the slip chain it will automatically open. If you should find that the slip chain is staying closed after you've pulled up and released it, you probably have the slip chain on upside down. Simply remove it, turn it over, and place it back on your dog's

Michael Kamer and "Aaron" demonstrating heeling position before "Sit."

neck.

Position the dog on your left side and put the loop of the leash on your right thumb. Double the leash so that the excess of the leash is out to your right side. Place your left hand down over the top of the leash so that you have both hands on the leash palms down and the dog is standing by your left side.

Michael Kamer and "Aaron" demonstrating "Heel-Sit" position.

place your thumb on one side and your forefinger on the other and squeeze ever so gently, your dog will tend to drop his rear end. This is a ticklish area to your puppy, much the same as it would be to you or me.

Now having your dog in a seated position, place your left hand back on the leash. As you step off on your left foot, you will call your dog by name and give the command "Heel," and begin to walk in a brisk manner. Each time you change direction, for example, a 45-degree turn to the right or a 45-degree turn to the left, you will repeat your dog's name and very briskly repeat the command "Heel."

Each and every time you stop, do so abruptly. As you come to a stop, release your left hand from the leash, pull up on the leash with your right hand, placing the left thumb and forefinger on the small of your dog's back, and push down saying, "Sit," in a bright tone of voice. The dog will learn to "sit" each and every time you come to a stop.

Once the dog is seated, place the left hand approximately two feet in front of his nose and say, "Stay." Then return your left hand to the leash and

Now we will begin the exercise.

Pull up on the slip chain with your right hand while your left hand straddles your dog's hindquarters just in front of his hips. You will find this area is rather soft and when you pause. Count to 20 or 30 quietly to yourself. This is recommended to avoid rushing, and your dog will learn to have patience and not to anticipate commands.

Repeat the exercise. If the dog lags, snap the leash forward. Another option is to step off, allowing your left thigh to come up, and snap the leash forward. If the dog lunges forward, turn and walk a few feet in the opposite direction. Once the dog is under control, return to the original direction of your walk, call your dog by name, and give the command "Heel." If at any time your dog wanders in front of you, nudge him out of the way with the top of the left calf,

Michael Kamer and "Aaron" demonstrating position of left hand for assisted "Sit and Heel."

left knee, or left thigh, depending on your dog's height and say, "Fido, Heel." Thus, your dog will learn to stay parallel to you whether you are turning or walking straight.

Remember each time that you stop to have your dog "Sit." Soon, the "Sit" will become automatic. At that point delete the voice command "Sit." Each time your dog does this exercise properly, pet him briskly and tell him, "Good boy!" This keeps the dog's spirits high and his interest piqued.

In all of our training we avoid as best possible the use of any negativity whatsoever and try to accentuate the positive so

Michael Kamer and "Sebastian" demonstrating left hand "Stay" signal.

This page: Use of left knee to make your dog off you during left turn.

as to keep the dog happy, alert and interested in what is being done. This exercise should be practiced 12–15 minutes, three to four times per day, as your schedule allows. When your dog achieves proficiency in this exercise, there will be no pressure between you and your dog on the leash as you walk or turn, and he will "sit" automatically when you stop.

"HEEL" and "SIT-STAY"

Repeat the heeling exercise and again come to a "Sit-Stay"; tell your dog to "Stay" with the left hand. Walk straight out to the end of the leash, place the loop of the leash on your left thumb, turn and face your dog. Repeat the "Stay" command with the right hand extended (as a

Right hand "Stay" signal.

policeman would stop traffic). If while you wait in this position your dog starts getting up, use the hand signal for "Sit" (an upward motion of the right hand) and then extend the right hand straight

Frontal correction for "Sit."

Frontal "Stay" correction.

Circling right exercise.

outward, repeating, "Stay." Each hand signal is capable of becoming a physical correction should it be necessary. "Sit" would become a correction by stepping in on the right leg, coming up underneath the leash with the right hand, pulling straight up (which throws your dog's weight to his rear and he will "Sit" once again), then rocking back on your right leg. Bring your legs parallel again and extend the right hand, and say "Stay." "Stay" would become a physical correction by stepping forward on the right leg, tapping your dog on the front of the nose, and then stepping back on the right leg.

Do this until you have gotten him to the point where he will remain in this position for a minute while you stand straight out directly away from the dog. Then signal "Stay" with the right hand and circle right around the dog, keeping the leash (on the point during your moving around, the dog starts to rise or lie down, immediately give the hand signal and voice command for "Sit" in a firm monotone. Should this not

Circling left exercise. (Note leash on right thumb). Left thumb is used for right circles.

left thumb) in front of the dog's face at all times. Next switch the leash to the right thumb and circle to the left, completely around the dog (keeping the leash in front of the dog's face at all times).

Return to your original position in front of your dog (face to face). If at any suffice, step in on your right leg, pulling up underneath the leash.

Follow this by the hand signal for "Stay" and if necessary "tap" on his nose as well. The importance of keeping the leash in front of the dog's face is so that your dog does not presume that you

Left circling exercise. (Note leash on right thumb). Left thumb is used for right circles.

want him to come with you as you circle. You will know this exercise has been proficiently accomplished when after telling your dog to "Heel," "Sit," and "Stay," you can walk out to the end of the leash and briskly circle the dog without his moving from the position. As you do this exercise, extend the period of time that your dog is in the "Sit-Stay"; two minutes is the optimum period. This exercise should be added to your dog's repertoire and practiced three to four times a day.

Review

Loop on the right thumb, palms down on the leash, say "Heel" and start to walk. Don't bend your head down, stand up straight. Don't wait for the dog and no premature jerking. When you stop and tell your dog to "Sit," if he leans on you, nudge him off. Then "Heel," turn left, turn right (saying your dog's name and "Heel" at each turn). Stop abruptly (say dog's name and "Sit"), wait a few seconds (say dog's name and "Stay"), walk out to the end of the leash, switch hands, face the dog and wait (say dog's name and "Stay"), circle him completely.

Pointers

Don't wait for the dog when you start the heeling exercise. If the dog has his bottom out to the left, circle to the left. If his bottom is in back of you, circle to the right. If the dog stops, still standing, with his bottom in back of you, tap his bottom with your right foot to coax the dog's bottom out to the left. Then follow through with "Sit." You must end up with the dog sitting parallel to you. Keep the left hand two to three feet from your dog's face when saying "Stay," so the dog isn't tempted to lick your hand.

"DOWN"

Down is the exercise where your dog is taught to lie flat down on the ground when told to do so from either a "Sit" or a "Stand" position. To start teaching your dog to lie down, have your dog in a heeling position on a "Sit-Stay" by your left side and

Michael Kamer and "Murphy" demonstrating beginning of "Down" exercise.

Beginning "Down" exercise by lifting left front foot off the ground.

tell him to "Stay" using your left hand; signal for "Stay." Then walk out in front of the dog approximately two feet, turn and face him. Place the leash folded in half into your left hand. Raise

Pull leash downward in the direction where left front foot would be if not lifted.

your right hand straight up above your head, and swinging your index finger briskly toward the ground, say to your dog, using your command tone of voice, "Down." Your dog will most likely not respond to this command since he doesn't know it. Repeat this trying to lever the dog into the "Down" position. It is simply being lifted up off the ground to keep it from supporting the dog on the left front portion of the dog's body. Now pull down gently on the slip chain with your left hand, and swing your dog over to the

"Stay" after achieving "Down" position.

procedure two or three times so that your dog has an opportunity to familiarize himself with this hand motion. Next, swing your right hand down toward the ground, saying, "Down," then pick up your dog's left front foot so that it is off the ground and hold it gently in your right hand. In no way is it to be used as a means of side where the foot is no longer supporting the dog, while saying "Down." Your dog will easily lie down since there is no support under that portion of his body. Once he has been brought into the "Down" position, release your right hand from your dog's left front foot, and extend it out in front of your dog's face about two feet and say

Beginning of "Come" exercise.

"Stay" briskly. Stand up straight, pause a moment, back off to the end of the leash and wait. This exercise should be followed by an approximately 20- to 30-second wait which will be increased over a period of time until your dog will remain in this "Down" position at least three minutes. Each time your dog completes this exercise successfully, praise him briskly with your hand and say, "Good boy, Good boy." Once your dog will do the "Down-Stay" position for at least three minutes, incorporate into this the complete circling used earlier in the "Sit-Stay" position, remembering always to keep your dog's leash directly in front of the dog's face so that he doesn't mistake the leash going around him for a cue to get up and come with you. Once you have circled completely left and right go back out to the end of the leash, facing your dog directly, pause, and then return to the heeling position.

"COME"

To begin teaching your dog to "Come," place your dog in the "Heel-Sit-Stay" position, then walk out to the end of the leash and stand and face your dog. Using a beckoning motion across your chest, tell your dog to "Come." Do this in a commanding tone of voice two or three times for each command, and use your dog's name in conjunction with the command. Example: ("Fido, Come! Fido, Come!"). Repeat this

three times to familiarize your dog with this hand-and-voice motion. After the three motions, tell your dog to "Come" and then

begin picking up the leash with the right hand and feeding it into the left hand, reeling in your dog as if you were reeling in a

Pulling up leash during "Come" exercise.

Preparing for "Sit" during "Come" exercise.

fish. Once your dog has gotten completely up in front of you, place both hands on the leash against your stomach. Then pull up toward your chest and

Frontal "Sit," completing "Come" exercise.

say, "Sit." This will make your dog drop his bottom immediately. Then tell your dog to "Stay" and praise him briskly. Move back out to the full end of the leash, repeat the hand signal two or three times ("Fido, Come! Fido, Come!") and briskly pick up the leash with the right hand, again feeding it into the left hand and placing both hands on the leash, once again pulling up toward the chest and saying, "Sit." This pull-up motion will make your dog tuck his rear under himself briskly

and sit close to you. It is important to note that your dog should be sitting close enough to you so that you can easily extend your right hand and place your palm on his forehead. For smaller dogs, you'll have to bend forward, but should you find yourself having to bend forward to reach an average-size dog, the dog likely needs to be closer to you. Once again move out to the end of the leash and repeat the command to "Come," but this time briskly walk backwards as you call your dog, giving the dog a sensation of coming to you over a greater distance. Then come to a brisk stop and reel in the leash, picking it up with the right hand and feeding it to the left. When your dog is close up to you this time, give an upward motion of your right hand to "Sit." Should your dog not "Sit" immediately, put the right hand on the leash as well and pull up with both hands toward your chest as previously described. Tell your dog to "Stay" and walk back out to the end of the leash. Once again call your dog; as you do so step back briskly, picking the leash up with your right hand so that the dog begins to close up the distance with you more quickly. If, as your dog approaches, you notice his rear end is too far to the left or the right, while the dog is still standing, use the instep of the appropriate foot to straighten out your dog's bottom, so that when he drops his rear he will in fact be sitting straight in front of you. Should the front of the dog's body be not directly in front of you, put both hands on the leash and pull the dog's head to the left or to the right, whichever is required to straighten up the front of the dog's body. Ultimately, when your dog is seated in front of you, he should be seated squarely in front of you, so that you and he are directly facing each other. Once again tell your dog to "Stay," then walk out to the end of the leash and pause a minute or two.

You can also integrate into this exercise circling right and circling left. This exercise as well should be repeated seven or eight times, alternating coming at a distance of six feet and sitting, and coming and jogging backwards and then picking up the leash so that the dog "Sits" squarely in front of you. When the dog has reasonably mastered this exercise, you will notice that once you have said, "Fido, Come," he will begin to stand up and come to you. If there is any hesitancy whatsoever,

Sit-square correction.

Emergency "Stay" exercise.

begin jogging backwards and snap the leash towards yourself saying, "Fido, Come!" again, gathering up the leash so that your dog will begin moving toward you more briskly. Once he comes close, have him "Sit" and "Stay" again. Once your dog has mastered this exercise, you will have noticed that you can say, "Fido, Come!" and your dog will briskly move up to you and sit.

Continue repeating this exercise seven or eight times in sequence and then break up that exercise by adding it to your other exercises, so that your dog now has a routine that takes approximately 15 minutes. The repertoire at this point should be practiced two or

three times a day, since the lesson duration has now been extended as the dog's interest span has increased.

Note: Do NOT accommodate the dog by moving toward him. Each time your dog does this exercise properly be sure to praise him briskly, both physically and verbally, saying, "Good boy, Good boy, Good dog!" and patting him.

EMERGENCY "STAY" AFTER RECALL

The purpose of this exercise is to teach your dog an emergency "Stay"; to teach your dog to freeze in place after you have called him in case of an emergency. Example: Should you have just called your dog, but now see a car coming down the street and wish to avoid an accident, an emergency "Stay" would be a necessary command. This teaches your dog to freeze in place at any point during the recall exercise. To begin this exercise, place your dog in the "Heel-Sit-Stay" position, walk out to the end of the leash and face your dog. Call your dog once or twice so that he briskly rises and comes directly to you and sits. Now tell the dog to "Stay" and again walk out to the end of the leash. Call your dog telling him to "Come." Briskly jog backwards after your dog has traversed approximately eight or nine feet, stop, extend the right hand in front of yourself and sharply say, "Fido, Stay!" This will surprise your dog and he will naturally freeze in place. Should he continue coming, step forward on your right foot, tap your dog on the front of the nose, and repeat the command "Stay". Then move fully back out to the end of the leash and repeat the recall exercise. This exercise of "Come-Stay, Come-Stay" should be practiced alternately with the full "Come" or

recall exercise so that your dog does not become apprehensive when you call him, always anticipating a "Stay" command. This exercise added to your repertoire will extend the duration of the lesson to approximately 18 minutes.

"DOWN TO SIT—SIT TO DOWN"

Start by putting your dog in a "Down-Stay" position. Tell your dog to "Sit" by using the "Sit"

Emergency "Stay" correction.

Emergency "Stay" command during "Come" exercise.

Demonstrating "Come" hand signal.

the tip of your shoe. This tapping will make your dog pull his foot back and thus "Sit." Once he has seated himself, tell him to "Stay." Allow your dog to stay in this position a minute or two. You are now prepared to repeat the "Down" exercise. Once again, raise the right hand above your head, swing it down toward the ground with the right index finger pointed downward. Do this two or three times, then lift up the dog's left front foot with your right hand while pulling the leash downward to return your dog to the "Down" position. Now tell him to "Stay." Repeat the "Down" to "Sit" exercise, and the "Sit" to "Down" exercise, seven or eight times. Then tell your dog to "Stay" while in the

hand signal, which is an upward motion of the right hand; repeat this command two or three times to familiarize your dog with that motion. Now repeat the hand motion for "Sit" with the right hand and gently lift up with the left hand on the leash while you tap either of your dog's front feet with

Demonstrating "Sit" hand signal.

Demonstrating "Sit" hand signal while tapping dog's foot.

"Down" position, walk out to the end of the leash, say "Stay," again using the hand signal. Now circle your dog completely to the right, keeping the leash on your left thumb and in front of his face. Once you have completed this circle, say "Stay" again with the right hand. Now place the loop of the leash on the right thumb, circle completely to the left until you are back in front of your dog, out at the end of

Demonstrating "Stay" hand signal.

Circling left, leash on right thumb.

alternate circling at the end of the set, once from the "Down" position circle, once from the "Sit" position circle. You will know your dog has accomplished this exercise when, from a distance of two or three feet in front of your dog, you can say "Down" and in one or two tries only using the hand signal and voice command the dog goes into that position. Thereafter, eliminate raising of the left front foot and simply use your hand signal and voice

the leash. Now fold the leash in half, walk back up to the front of the dog until you are approximately two feet from him. Repeat the "Down" to "Sit" exercise and the "Sit" to "Down" exercise again seven or eight times. Then walk out to the end of the leash; when your dog is in a "Sit" position circle right, then circle left. Repeat this exercise another seven or eight times, followed by the circling to the right or the left from the "Down." Then

Keep leash in front of the dog's face to avoid him following you.

command. If the dog at any point seems apprehensive about lifting the left front foot off the ground, simply pull on the leash to indicate the "Down" position. At this point in his progress, this should be all that is necessary to complete the exercise.

In regard to sitting from the "Down" position, you will know your dog has

Circling right (note the leash kept in front of the dog's face).

Demonstrating "Sit" from three feet away.

"Sit" hand signal while tapping the dog's foot.

accomplished this exercise when you are a distance of two or three feet from your dog, and using only the hand signal for "Sit" and voice command, your dog goes into the "Sit" position. If he appears to start the exercise and is hesitant, fake coming forward with your foot to the dog's toe (don't actually tap the foot at this point), and if the dog goes up into the "Sit" position, you will know that he understands the exercise but simply feels like trying you. Add this exercise to your dog's repertoire of "Heel," "Sit," and "Stay," so that the routine now includes everything he has already learned and this new exercise. At this point, the training period will probably be extended to about 20 minutes each session. The repertoire should be practiced three 20-minute sessions per day. Pet and praise your dog by telling him, "Good boy! Good boy!" when each session is over.

"STAND"

To begin the "Stand" exercise, place your dog in the initial "Heel-Sit-Stay" position, giving the hand signal for "Stay" with the

left hand as in prior lessons. Walk out in front of your dog about two or three feet and place the folded leash in your left hand. Tell your dog "Stand" using the appropriate hand signal,

This page: Demonstrating "Stand" hand signal. Open and close hand repeatedly.

"Stand" hand signal while walking toward rear foot.

which is a wiggling of the fingers of the right hand while your arm remains at your right side—palm facing out—bend your fingers to your palm. Repeat this two or three times to familiarize your dog with this hand motion, then proceed to nudge either of your dog's back feet with the tip of your shoe, the same way you nudged one of his front feet for the "Sit" exercise. This will make your dog want to lift up his rear and move his back feet away from your foot. When beginning this exercise, the leash should be taut. Once the dog starts to raise himself into the "Stand" position, slack off on the leash a bit so that he can have some room in which to move up into the "Stand" position. Once the dog is in the "Stand-Stay" position, allow him to stand there for a minute or two. Then, giving the dog the hand signal for "Sit," which is an upward motion of the right hand. He should immediately drop his rear end. If he does not, use the correction for "Sit," which is an upward motion of the right hand coming up underneath the leash as you step in on the right leg for leverage and

"Stand" hand signal while tapping rear foot.

snap up and say, "Sit." Then rock back on your right leg and tell your dog to "Stay." Repeat the command for "Stand," wiggling the right-hand fingers, two or three times and then nudge either of right hand up into the "Sit" position and tell your dog "Sit." When your dog starts to understand this exercise, you will notice that the dog begins to get up into the "Stand" position as you say it. If

Demonstrating "Stand" hand signal from end of leash (six feet).

your dog's back feet with the foot closest to that side of his body (left side of body, right foot; right side of body, left foot). Do not cross your feet over as this may put you off-balance. Nudge the dog's foot with the tip of your foot and the dog once again will "Stand." As he rises, slack off on the leash to give him room to move up into the "Stand." Once he is in the "Stand" position, allow him to stay there a minute or two, praise your dog with a pat and a "Good boy!" Then, again swing the

there should be any hesitancy at this point, fake stepping forward on the appropriate foot to nudge your dog's foot and you will see the dog has discerned that it's time to get up. Repeat this exercise seven or eight times and praise your dog, and then move into one of the exercises that your dog knows well.

A point should be made at this time that any time a new exercise is added into the dog's repertoire, you should practice it for seven or eight repetitions

Completed "Stand" exercise.

"Down" hand signal.

INTEGRATING "STAND" WITH "DOWN" AND "SIT"

Place your dog in a "Sit-Stay" position, give him the appropriate hand signal for "Stay" with the left hand. Stand two to three feet from the dog, placing the leash folded in your left hand. Tell your dog "Down" followed by "Stay" and pause for two minutes. Walk back out to the end of the leash, circle to the right 360 degrees with the loop of the leash on your left thumb, return to your position in front of the dog, repeat the command "Stay" with the right hand, place the loop of the leash on the right thumb, circle left until you are back in front of the dog. Tell your dog to "Sit," "Stay," and circle right,

and then move into other exercises that the dog has already accomplished.

Once the dog has a reasonably proficient understanding of this exercise, it can be integrated with the "Sit" and "Down" exercise as follows.

"Stay" hand signal while dog is in "Down" position.

circle left. Tell your dog "Stand," "Stay," circle right, circle left. Tell your dog "Down" from the "Stand" position. If there is any hesitation, snap downward on the leash and the dog will go into the "Down" position; should there be any further hesitancy, raise the dog's left front foot with your right hand pulling the dog downward with the leash. As you practice this exercise over a period of days, increase the distance you are from your dog until you are fully out at the end of your six-foot leash. At that point, you should be able to tell your dog to "Sit," "Stay," and circle right, circle left. "Down," "Stay," circle right, circle left. "Sit," "Stay," and circle right, circle left. "Stand," "Stay," and circle right, circle left.

Correction for not lying down. Snap leash toward ground while saying "Down."

"Down" correction snapping leash toward ground while saying, "Down."

"Sit" hand signal.

"Stay" hand signal with dog in "Stand" position.

"Down" from the "Stand" to the "Stay," and circle right, circle left. You should be able to integrate this exercise with your "Heeling" now and have your dog go into a "Sit-Down" or a "Stand" from any of the other positions while you are out at the end of the leash.

"FINISH"

The "Finish" is the exercise in which your dog is taught, after he has been called up to you and is seated squarely in front of you, upon the command of "Heel" to raise himself up, circle around behind you from right to left, come up to your left side and sit in the original heeling

position. The exercise is taught in the following manner. Place your dog in the initial "Heel-Sit-Stay" position, walk out to the full extent of the leash, face your dog squarely, call him to you by name using the appropriate hand signal across your chest—your dog should briskly come up to you and seat himself squarely. Then fold the leash into your right hand, tell your dog, "Fido, Heel!" and fake stepping back on your right foot as you gently pull back on your right arm. The purpose of this movement is to give your dog the sense that you're moving to your right when you say "Heel." After repeating this

Demonstrating proximity of dog on "Come" before telling dog to "Sit."

Demonstrating step back on "Finish" exercise to convey direction in which dog is to circle.

Dog arriving at left side after circling behind you and preparing to sit.

familiarization exercise two or three times, step back fully on your right foot and pull back briskly on your right arm. This will make your dog rise and move around you to your right. As he begins to do so, take a full step forward on your right foot and bring up your left foot. As you do so, switch hands with the leash behind your back, bring your dog fully up to your left side, and have him "Sit."

Dog completing circle behind you and sitting.

Note: If your dog tends to lag, take two or three steps forward after you have pulled back, which will give your dog an increased period of time in which to get around your body. This will result in your dog's learning that he is to come around your body and line his shoulders up with your leg

"Aaron" circling behind while trainer is stepping back to convey direction while switching hands so that dog can complete the circling.

Stepping back on right foot conveys direction in which dog is to circle. (Note leash has now been put into left hand.)

Completed
"Finish."

by fully stepping back on your right foot, pulling back on your right arm, and switching hands with the leash behind your back. Take a full step forward on your right foot, bringing up your left foot, and as you do so switch hands with the leash behind your back. Bring the dog up to your left side and have him "Sit." Each time the dog completes this exercise praise him briskly, both physically and verbally. This exercise as well should be practiced seven or eight times, followed by integration with other exercises of the dog's repertoire. Continue to keep the lesson duration at 30 minutes for the time being, so that your dog's repertoire is completely covered in a 30-minute period with approximately five to ten minutes spent specifically on the newest exercise.

before he sits.

The purpose of the stepping back and stepping forward is to give your dog some initial time as well as space in which to complete a U-turn behind your body. Then tell your dog to "Stay" with the left hand and wait 30–40 seconds. Turn and face him, and move fully out to the end of the leash. Give the dog the recall command, using his name, and have him briskly come up to you and "Sit." Follow this by folding the leash in the right hand. Fake the movement back on your right foot and pull back on your leash two or three times, followed once again

"GO TO YOUR PLACE"

For your dog to have "His place" is very convenient, and the piece of carpeting or bedding you choose can be located where you wish it to be and moved as necessary.

you again away from the area, making a 180-degree turn. Walk back to the area and coax the dog forward with your left hand as you close on the area, saying, "Go to your place." As you practice this, you will find that as your dog nears his area, he will begin to understand that you want him to go ahead of you to that place; he will do so, and "Sit" and "Stay." As you see your dog comprehend this exercise, of course praise him briskly. In addition, increase the distance in which you stop from the area, so that ultimately you could be anywhere

This exercise is accomplished in much the same way as the exercise of having the dog get in and out of the car. In this exercise you will "Heel" him briskly to his carpeting or area and as you arrive at it have him go ahead of you a step or two, coaxing him forward with your left hand from the "Heel," and say "Go to your place." Have him "Sit" and "Stay," drop the leash, walk away about five to ten feet and pause. Return to your dog, praise him briskly, and have him "Heel" with

Dog now lying on his "Place" in "Down-Stay" position.

Dog being told "Down-Stay" after having arrived at "Place."

within a reasonable distance of 15, possibly 20 feet and be able to tell your dog "Go to your place!", and your dog will seek out his area and "Sit" or "Lie Down" on it.

"HEAD UP"

"Head up" is an exercise we recommend for dogs that have a propensity for dropping their heads either in the "Sit-Stay" position or the "Down-Stay" position on a

continuous or regular basis. Each time you see your dog dropping his head, you will say "Head up!" Briskly put your hand under his lower jaw, push upwards, and raise the head up where you want it. Follow that with the voice command and hand signal for "Stay." Circle

correctly. Ultimately this correction will eliminate that problem.

DROP LEASH

Once you and your dog have accomplished the basic repertoire of obedience commands to a degree of proficiency, it will be time to commence

Demonstrating head-up correction.

around your dog in both directions and you will find that the dog will begin to pay closer attention to you. Practice the "Head up" routine from the "Down" position, the "Sit" position, and the "Stand" position. You will find that within a matter of days, each time your dog starts to drop his head, your command of "Head up!" will bring the response of his holding his head up

the drop leash portion of training.

Place your dog by your side in the heeling position in a "Sit-Stay," hold your leash in the normal manner, start to walk, and as you say "Heel," slap your left hip with your left hand and step off. Once you and your dog are moving, place the entire leash in your left hand and place your left hand in the small of your back.

Demonstrating left hand is in small of your back when starting drop-leash "Heeling."

"Heel." Continue the heeling exercise for approximately three or four minutes, and then come to an abrupt stop. As you do so, raise your *right* hand in front of your dog's face in a 90-degree motion, giving the "Sit" signal. Your dog, seeing this hand signal, will recognize it as one that's been used before and will stop abruptly and sit. Should your dog continue, however, step on the leash with your left foot and repeat the hand signal again. Once your dog has seated himself, say, "Stay" to your dog and use the left hand now for a hand signal, making sure that your hand is at least two or three feet in front of his nose to preclude licking and playing. Pick up the leash, walk out to the end,

As you walk briskly ahead, say "Heel" and turn 90 degrees to the right. If your dog lags, give him a slight snap forward and say, "Heel." If your dog leads, give him a slight snap back and say, "Heel." Once you have made two right turns and proceed to make two left turns, very quietly drop the leash that you've been holding in your hand in the small of your back. Continue walking at the same pace; at this point, however, each time you make a turn you slap your left hip, call your dog by name and say, drop it at your feet, step back approximately a foot from the leash, and put your dog through the routine you normally would use when you're in front of him. First tell your dog, "Down," swinging your right hand down to the ground very dramatically. If your dog fails to go "Down," step in on the right foot, grasp the leash that's laying at your feet with your right hand, give a gentle snap, and say, "Down." Step back, stand up straight, pause and say, "Stay," extending the right hand out in front of your body. Next give the hand signal for "Sit," a 90-degree upward motion of the right hand, and tell your dog to "Sit." Should your dog fail to sit, step in, nudge either of the dog's front feet with the tip of one of your shoes and say, "Sit." If this should fail, grasp the leash, pull upward, say, "Sit" followed by "Stay," then drop the leash again. Step back to the end of the leash, so that you're approximately one foot away from it, and tell your dog to "Stand," using the appropriate hand signal of wiggling the

Leash dropped, "Heeling" is continued. Slap your left thigh each time you change direction.

Leash dropped while in stationary position. Thigh is slapped as you step off for advanced drop-leash "Heel."

Moving slapped thigh and repeating voice command of "Heel" each time you turn.

Loose-leash heeling pre-requesite to drop leash.

Each time you stop have your dog "Sit."

fingers of your right hand. If your dog fails to stand, step in briskly, nudge either of his rear feet with either of your feet (keeping the left foot for the dog's right side, and the right foot for the dog's left side), so that your dog stands. Step back until you're one foot from the end of the leash.

Repeat this routine in any sequence you desire, "Sit," "Stand," and "Down," until it is apparent that your dog understands what you mean, and responds consistently while you are at least a foot from the end of the leash. Next tell your dog to "Come"; your dog will get up and briskly come up in front of you. Give the upward motion of the right hand for "Sit" and say, "Sit." Should your dog fail to respond to this command, bend over, pick up the leash, give a gentle snap on it and say, "Come"; now jog back approximately two to three feet, stopping abruptly so that your dog gets the concept of moving toward you. Repeat this exercise for approximately 10 to 15 minutes, until it's apparent that your dog understands that when you say "Come," even though the leash is not in your hand, he is to trot over to you and "Sit." Once your dog has mastered this exercise, then include the "Emergency-Stay." Always remember to do approximately seven or eight full recall exercises and then interject one or two "Come Emergency-Stay" exercises. I recommend this to prevent your dog from anticipating the emergency stay and slowing down the tempo that he comes to you. Next we will work on the finish exercise in the drop leash fashion. Drape the leash to your right and drop it

Drop-leash "Sit" hand signal with right hand.

on the ground, slap your right hip, and say, "Heel." Step back on it simultaneously and your dog will see this motion, get up and start to pass your right side. Step forward one full step and slap your left hip, repeating the

Demonstrating "Sit" hand signal from "Heel" position.

command to "Heel" and your dog will complete the semi-circle. As soon as your dog's front shoulders are parallel with your left leg, give him the upward motion of the right hand for the "Sit" command. Then praise him briskly for having responded appropriately. Should he fail to do this, reach down to the ground, pick up the dropped leash with your right hand, step back on the right leg, slap your hip and give the dog a gentle tug. As soon as the dog starts to move, drop the leash, step forward one full step, slap your left hip and your dog should

complete the half-circle and begin to sit by your left side as you give the upward motion.

The preceding exercises should be practiced in a routine approximately 15 or 20 minutes per session, two to three times per day. At this point slap your left hip, start to "Heel," and walk with your dog, leaving the leash dropped on the ground. Pick up the leash only if your dog fails to understand or respond appropriately by beginning to walk with you. As you practice this procedure, two or three times per day, 15 to 20 minutes per session, you will find that

Stepping back and slapping right thigh to start off-leash "Finish" exercise.

your dog's proficiency will increase. Once it is apparent that your dog understands all of his commands from the drop-leash position, with you at least one foot from the leash when working him, it will be time to commence the off-leash procedure.

OFF-LEASH TRAINING

Now that your dog has accomplished proficiency in drop-leash routines, it is time to commence off-leash. Place your dog in the initial heeling position by your left side, in a seated position with the leash held in your hand. Slap your left leg, start to walk, and while saying "Heel," make one or two right turns. Repeat the command "Heel" and be sure that you precede the command by your dog's name. Make a couple of left turns in the same manner, and then a couple of about-turns. At this point, reach over to the snap of the leash and gently remove it. Now carry the leash in your left hand, so that your dog is no longer connected to the leash but can still sense that the leash is present. Continue the heeling routine, turning left, turning right, turning about, for at least another three to four minutes. Now come to an abrupt stop, raise your right hand in front of the dog's face, and tell him to "Sit." Switch hands with the leash, and place it in your right hand. With your left hand open in front of his face about two or three feet, deliver the command to "Stay." Walk out in front of your dog approxi-mately five or six feet, raise your right hand above your head, and tell your dog, "Down." If he fails to lie down, step in grasping the loose ring of the slip chain, and gently snap it down. Next tell your dog to "Sit," raise the right hand into the 90- degree position and repeat the command "Sit." Should your dog fail to do so, correct him by nudging either front foot with one of your feet. Next use the command "Stand" and your dog should stand up on all four feet. Should he fail to stand, use the appro-priate correction, namely nudging either of his back feet with one of yours. Repeat this exercise, "Sit" to "Stand," "Stand" to "Down," "Down" to "Sit" or "Stand," for approxi-mately four to five minutes. Then back up approxi-mately six or seven feet and tell your dog to "Come." Your dog should briskly come to you and sit; if he does not, use the upward motion for the "Sit" command. Should he fail to come, step up to

Stepping back and slapping right thigh to start off-leash "Finish" exercise.

Heeling off leash. Dog, however, can see the leash.

"Heel." He should get up and begin to circle behind you. Next slap the left hip and say "Heel." He should complete his semi-circle and sit by your side. If at any point along this juncture, your dog hesitates or pauses, simply grasp the loose ring of the slip chain and give it a gentle pull to complete the exercise. This complete off-leash routine should be practiced 15 to 20 minutes per session, two to three times per day.

him, grasp the loose ring of the slip chain, give a gentle pull toward you, and say, "Come." As soon as your dog starts to move, trot backwards for at least a distance of five or six feet. Once your dog has grasped this concept, have him sit in front of you, place the leash in your right hand, slapping your right hip with the right hand (with the leash in it), step back on it and tell your dog to

Preparing to stop while heeling off leash.

TROUBLE SHOOTING

If you find you have any particular problems with your dog and any of these off-leash procedures, I suggest using a six- or seven-foot length of nylon parachute cord or buy a lightweight nylon leash, and tying it to the D-ring, using a lightweight leash the distance from which your dog will respond to his commands until you can regularly anticipate his responding proficiently from at least 15 to 20 feet. At this juncture, you will know your dog thoroughly understands off-leash responsiveness.

dropped on the ground. Your dog generally will not sense that it is on him, and it will enable you to initiate any necessary correction immediately. Once it has become apparent that your dog understands an exercise that before he did not, eliminate the parachute cord or leash. Over a period of weeks, increase

SEPARATING VOICE COMMANDS AND HAND SIGNALS

Now that your dog has successfully completed off-leash exercises, it is time to separate voice commands and hand signals. Our goal is that your dog can respond proficiently to hand signals, voice commands, or both. Start by putting

Advanced off-leash "Stay" at 15 feet. Hand signal only.

your dog through the off-leash routine by using his name and verbal commands. If at any juncture in an exercise, it appears that your dog is hesitant or not comprehending, add the confusion, incomprehension or stubbornness, repeat the exercise with the hand signal. This routine should be practiced 15 to 20 minutes per day, two to three times per day. Once

Off-leash "Down." Hand signal only.

hand signal. For example, if you have said "Down" to your dog two or three times in a firm command tone of voice and the dog seems perplexed or stubborn, add the hand signal and tell your dog to lie down. Using the appropriate command, and the appropriate exercise, put your dog through the entire off-leash routine, using only verbal commands. At any juncture if the dog fails to respond, either because of

it is apparent to you that your dog understands the verbal command alone, it is time to commence responsiveness to hand signals alone.

Let's start with the "Heel." Slap your left hip and start to walk, and as you make turns, repeat the slap. When you come to a stop, give the upward motion of the right hand. Continue practicing this exercise for approximately five or six minutes, and alternate giving and not giving the sit hand signal, until we get to a point where your dog will sit automatically, responding to the hand signal or the voice command. Then give your dog the hand signal for "Stay" with the left hand, walk out seven or eight feet from your dog, and employ the off-leash routine using hand signals alone. If at any juncture your dog appears to be stubborn, perplexed, or confused, simply add in the voice command as you repeat the exercise— eliminate the voice command as soon as your dog understands this exercise. Continue practicing this routine until your dog will respond to hand signals alone throughout the off-leash routine.

You can now congratulate yourself, because you have a very proficiently trained dog, who will respond knowingly on-leash and off-leash to a combination of voice commands and hand signals, or to either hand signals or voice commands alone.

Congratulations to both you and your dog! I'm very proud of you!

SMALL DOG TECHNIQUE

When working with a small or short dog, I have found that initially it is very handy to practice certain exercises that are taught in this course from a table top. This saves many elderly folks or people with back problems the effort of having to bend over or down repeatedly in the initial process of teaching the dog a new technique or behavior.

REPRIMAND/CORRECTION

Each hand signal is capable of becoming a physical reprimand should the dog fail to respond in the initial training to the hand signal–voice combination.

"Stay" would become a physical correction by stepping forward on the right leg, tapping your dog on the front of the nose, and then stepping back on the right leg.

The hand signal for

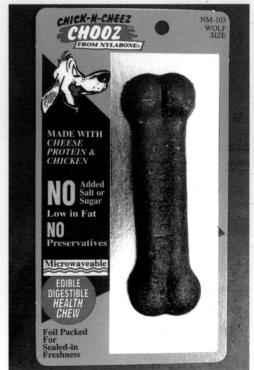

"Stay" would become a physical reprimand by extending the right hand with a gentle tap on the nose.

"Sit" would become a correction by stepping in on the right leg, coming up underneath the leash with the right hand, pulling straight up (which throws your dog's weight to his rear and he will sit once

the right hand to throw your dog's weight to his rear and make him seat himself.

QUESTION: If my dog walks away from the spot I told him to "Sit" at, is it important to take him back to the same spot?

ANSWER: Yes, if he started to get up and you caught him in the act of getting up, he would in

Correction for not sitting. Step in on right leg while pulling up on leash with right hand.

again) then rocking back on your right leg, bringing your legs parallel again, and extending the right hand and saying "Sit."

The hand signal for "Sit" would become a physical reprimand by stepping in on the right leg and pulling up underneath the leash with

fact be in the same spot. If you were tardy in getting that correction to him and he had advanced two or three feet, YES, you would go up to him and, using your "Heel" (which means he's on your left side), you would take him abruptly back to where he was. The psychology being, you try to avoid as much correcting and reprimanding as possible, and the best way to do that is to "nip in the bud" anything he begins to do wrong.

The hand signal for "Come," the beckoning motion across the chest, would become a reprimand by grasping the leash with the right hand and reeling in the dog with the leash in your left hand.

If your dog "Comes" before the command is given, tell him, "No! Bad dog!" "Heel" him back to where he was. Heeling is always on the left side of your body. Tell the dog to "Stay" and then wait. If the dog is out of line when you ask him to "Come," you correct the front of the dog by pulling the leash in the direction you need him to go. You would correct the rear of the dog by using your instep closest to the hip you need to line up. Example: He is leaning over on the left side, you would say, "Sit," and you would nudge him to the right with your left foot. We want him to know that when you say "Come," he's got to be right there in front of you and sitting squarely.

"Down"; The hand signal for "Down" would become a reprimand by stepping in on the right leg and pulling down with the

Pulling up on leash for "Sit" while dog is in front of you.

right hand on top of the leash toward the ground.

Next say "STAY" and circle him. Go back to his side for heeling. Dog's right side so that you would go back to the right side of the dog. Recover the leash, palms down with the loop on the right thumb. Start to walk and say "Heel." Pull him up when lagging. Each time you change direction, repeat the command, say your dog's name, and say "Heel." When you see his bottom coming in, it's the time to nudge him back

Pushing dog's rear out with right foot behind left leg.

chain, and pushing down with your left hand, straddling the dog's hindquarters firmly and saying, "Sit." It is most essential that your hand signals be clear and direct and that your voice commands be a good firm monotone as well. The rough or demonstrative dog needs to be told in so many words, "The party's over young man, now school is beginning." When the dog sees that this attitude is going to be projected throughout the lessons as well as in your daily living, he begins to acquiesce and in a matter of time becomes quite pliable and obedient in his training. It seems that a young dog's dogmatic approach that was used before to thwart his owners is now directed into prompt responses to commands.

out with the right foot behind the left leg. It's much easier to move your dog when he is still up on his feet than when he has seated himself.

When you start walking with him, don't give him a jerk as you say "Heel." We want him to follow your leg, sooner or later we will have that leash off. Instead of a forewarning pull, you say, "Heel," and start to walk.

Now, when you tell your puppy to "Heel," stop and say "Sit." This time you will be pulling directly up on the leash and slip

QUESTION: What do I do if my dog bolts forward when heeling?

ANSWER: A sharp snap on the leash would be

directed, coupled with the command "No!", followed by "Heel." A 180-degree change of direction would also occur to surprise the dog. This type of correction tends to make the dog realize that he must begin watching you very carefully, because he doesn't know when you may suddenly change direction. In addition, when such a dog finds that he can "get away with something" and that his owner will not effectively correct him for it, this rapidly becomes a habit with him and he is very stubborn about relinquishing an incorrect privilege that he has taken.

If your dog, for example, has found that when you're not in the room he can get up and sit on the couch, and that as a rule you may say, "No, no, bad dog," but go about what you were doing, the dog will quickly learn that your corrections are hollow. Your dog must believe you mean what you say!

Rewarding your dog with his favorite chew toy is an effective praise techique. This Border Terrier loves his Gumabone® Dental Device (made by Nylabone®). Photograph by Karen Taylor.

Personalities

STUBBORN DOGS

In dealing with the stubborn dog, we find that stubbornness must be met with stubbornness. For example, if you were to tell your "stubborn" dog to "Sit" and he were to get up, you must place the dog back in the "Sit-Stay" position repeatedly. Calmly, with a stern monotone voice and a direct upward pull on the leash with the right hand and slip chain, push down firmly on the hindquarters with your left hand straddling his rear.

A similar response can be used in dealing with the stubborn dog's nuisance problem. For example, if the dog were to dig a hole, by using our appropriate correction for digging you would show him the hole and tell him, "Bad dog!" Take him to the reprimand area on his leash (making sure, of course, he is in the shade). Once the hole is filled and leveled, wait approximately 15 to 20 minutes, return with the dog to the area, again scold the dog and tell him, "Bad dog!" If you were to find that your "stubborn" dog once again has dug, increase the period of time that your dog is being reprimanded (put on a chain leash and a leather collar) by 15-minute increments until you find that your dog complies. Dogs are very patient creatures. I have found that time passes for them a lot more quickly than it does for us, so a 10 or 15 minute period might seem like a long time for you, and most of us, suffering from childhood guilt anyway, feel that we are being cruel and "inhumane. " This truly is not the case. You will find that for the dog this time passed rather quickly.

Stubborn, rough and/or demonstrative dogs of average intelligence do require a firmer tone of voice, a firmer hand in training, and a very dogmatic, direct attitude from the owner. An owner who has difficulties with assertion would be well advised to stay away from rough, stubborn, or demonstrative dogs. However, in my estimation, with proper training they turn out to be very fine animals, and enjoy being given limits. I have found in my many years of teaching—both dogs and children are very similar in this area. Most children want limits and feel much happier when they know just how far they can go. The rough, stubborn, or demonstrative dog will tend to push as he would in the pack for leadership, until such time as the owner clearly takes control.

BRIGHT DOGS

Hopefully you are one of those dog owners who, with some knowledge and luck, selected a very bright dog. If he is bright as well as easygoing, God has blessed you. Dogs of this type are an absolute pleasure to train and they basically learn and pick up things as quickly as you teach them. They enjoy interaction with their owners and other people, children and other animals. These dogs are generally outgoing, very calm, and observant as well. You will notice with this type of dog that there is always a considerable amount of eye contact and facial expression. This type of dog not only enjoys general obedience work but also is an excellent candidate for advanced obedience and trick training. Consider yourself very fortunate and blessed if this is the "little critter" who has entered your home.

Akita pup showing interest in toy ball. One indication of intelligence is curiosity.

MODERATELY BRIGHT DOGS

We'll next deal with the puppies that are unfortunately less bright and may be more easily confused. These types of dogs are generally very sweet and cuddly, to some degree because they are insecure. That insecurity

Leonberger "Aaron" contemplating his day.

comes out of the fact that they are not quite sure what's going on some of the time, sometimes all of the time. I jokingly refer to this type of character as a dog who is in "constant contemplation." The best way to deal with this kind of personality is with a gentle, calm and assuring manner. This type of puppy or dog needs support, coaxing, consistent accommodations and much praise for the least of his successes. Such sensitivity and praise will result in effectively teaching the dog; what might be easy for other dogs is more difficult for them and learning begins to build their ego and self-confidence. They not only begin to feel better about themselves but also begin to feel very good about your support and assistance in their development. Anything at all that you can do to encourage this pup's ego, confidence, and perseverance is highly recommended. The slightest of victories should be rewarded with great praise and support. With time and patience, these puppies can master the content of basic training and be wonderful, loving pets. They do require patient, calm and understanding owners.

BRIGHT AND STUBBORN DOGS

Woe be unto you if you have chosen a bright and stubborn pup, because you're really going to have your work cut out for you. Not only is your dog stubborn and determined he's also got brains! This type of personality will test you regularly and will tempt your patience until you're ready to pull your hair out of your head! However, with perseverance, direct firm correction, consistent discipline, and regular daily practice sessions, this personality too can adjust to your lifestyle. They generally require regular review as

they will periodically continue to test you—after all, God has blessed them with exceptional intelligence. They also tend to be very precocious and constantly curious. I recommend this kind of pup for people with a great deal of patience, a great deal of stability and personality, and a lot of free time. Obviously, this type of dog will require more reinforcement than other personalities. Remember that with perseverance and patience this puppy too can be trained.

Dog owner James Edwards with his companion "Buddha," who has successfully completed "On" and "Off" leash obedience.

Maintenance

FOOD

Nowadays there is a plethora of dog foods and supplements available to the public. I believe that many of them are very good and very comparable. I've also learned that price does not necessarily equate with quality in dog foods; some of the finest quality dog foods sell for less than other brands which I personally would not use in my school. My recommendation is to read the label on the dog food, whether it be dry or canned, noting the content of the food, specifically the ingredients. If you find that the food seems to have more filler than other dog foods, it has a low percentage of protein and I would consider looking on. You will find that quality dog foods are comparable both in content and percentage of content. If you should find your dog has an adverse reaction to it, such as loose stool, flatus, constipation or an allergic reaction, definitely stop the food and consult your veterinarian. In my experience I have probably seen and used most dog foods available today, and most of the quality dog foods are pretty consistent in their ability to give most dogs what is needed for proper weight and coat conditioning. However, occasionally you will find that a particular food agrees well with one dog may not do so well with another. In this area we strongly recommend consulting both with the breeder of your puppy and your veterinarian. There are a number of snacks on the market nowadays for puppies, some of which are very fine, others which are totally valueless nutritionally. Our recommendation as educators is that between-meal snacks should be avoided entirely until it is apparent your new puppy is totally housebroken. There is absolutely no point in giving ammunition to a little fellow who's still in the process of being housebroken. However, once the housebreaking has been totally accomplished, I do recommend giving dogs an occasional snack such as a dog biscuit. There are a number of good quality brands on the market which act not only as roughage for your dog but also as a cleaning abrasive for his teeth. However, treats for dogs can be overdone much the same as they can for people, which I think accounts for a lot of the obesity we see in dogs nowadays. Do your dog a favor—keep the treats to a reasonable level. We recommend CHOOZ® to our readers. These chicken and cheese treats are available at pet shops all over. For a dog, body weight and conditioning are every bit as important as they are for us humans. An obese dog will have stress on his heart and respiratory system just the same as we, and it will result in poor health and a shorter life expectancy for the dog. We DO NOT recommend adding table leftovers to a dog's foods, since there are

"Baby Face Nelson" leaping to catch a ball.

a number of spices that we humans both use and abuse our systems with and a dog's system as a whole is not acclimated to these spices. Many times, in trying to be nice by providing your dog with a treat, you can very easily

spend a great deal of time in doing nothing, of course resulting in poor physical condition. If you are an apartment dweller, we recommend a brisk walk for your dog at least twice a day, and if you are fortunate enough to live in

A fine, fit, healthy Bull Terrier.

end up giving your dog an upset stomach.

EXERCISE

Exercise is just as important for dogs as it is for humans, since obesity is probably one of the biggest adversaries of the citified dog. Most dogs in a urban situation tend to

a home with a sizable backyard or near a park, we suggest exercising him there at least twice a day. Exercise helps stimulate your dog's respiratory system and his heartbeat. A healthy exercise routine coupled with an appropriately balanced diet will ensure your dog

"T.J.," a very healthy and fit Australian Cattle Dog owned by the author.

greater longevity. Interestingly enough, I have seen a number of different exercising tools for dog's, such as treadmills; however, I personally feel there's just something to be said about a nice brisk walk with your dog along the beach or in the park. Other than the obvious physical benefits of this exercise, I think it also enables you to have that special quality time that bonds you and your dog together. Speaking for myself, I for many years enjoyed walking with my dog in our neighborhood in the evenings for relaxation as well as exercise. Whenever I had the opportunity, I took him down to the beach for a romp in the surf and some special time alone.

I think we say many things to our dogs without words. My own personal dog is an Australian Cattle Dog, named T.J. I don't mind pointing out that T.J. stands for Tubbs Jr.; his dad's name is Tubbs, and Yes! You've got it! He is Tubbs Sr. T.J. has an ability to communicate with me, and I with him, through eye contact as well as the slightest nuances of my hand. I really don't think I'm any different than most dog owners in that I feel he and I have a very special relationship, and that having spent considerable time together, we know each other quite well. I must confess that he's one of my best listeners—he never talks back! And although I don't believe he understands each and every one of the words I use in a sentence, he's become quite versed in understanding the intonations in my statements as well as in picking up on my feelings. Some people might call that reading your vibrations or understanding your aura; I just call it good communication between a dog and his owner, and consider myself quite fortunate to have a relationship such as this with such a great dog.

HEALTH

The key to a healthy dog is your being aware of any changes in your dog's daily routine, especially his bathroom and eating habits. Usually one of the first signs of an unwell dog is that he will be off his regular feeding schedule. Other signs, such as loose stool, constipation, lethargy, or obvious pain, clearly indicate that it's time for a visit to the veterinarian. I also recommend at least twice a year, having a sample of your dog's stool checked for parasites. With as many places as our dogs get to go to these days, as well as with the contact they make with other animals, whether birds, a cat in your backyard or other dogs in the neighborhood, it's very possible for your dog to pick up a parasite simply by walking over a surface where another dog has eliminated. The biannual checking of a stool sample can catch any parasite your dog may have picked up before it becomes a particular problem. In addition, I recommend a physical for your dog at least once a year. This can be scheduled when your dog is due for regular booster shots. In regard to vaccinations, depending on the area you live in, the veterinarian will recommend the appropriate shots to keep your dog from picking up viruses or other contagious diseases that are known to be in that area. Most of these shots have a particular range of protection, ranging from six months to two-and-a-half years. It is very important to keep a record of these inoculations, as well as the appropriate time for boosters for the respective inoculations, so that your dog's protection is secured. One health tip I might mention to travellers: I recommend taking along the food that your dog is used to, and if at all possible the water he is used to. Many times a change of food or water can result in throwing his bowels off and upsetting his body metabolism. This can all be avoided by simply taking along what he's used to eating and drinking.

"T.J." retrieving his ball.

GROOMING

Grooming is a very necessary and important part of your dog's well-being. It is an opportunity to have some quality time with your new dog on an ongoing basis, as well as a means to keep your dog's coat and skin healthy. We recommend beginning your dog's grooming education when he is tired or sleepy. This way the puppy is not full of energy and does not feel particularly mischievous. If you have a puppy that tends to want to play with the grooming implements, take them out of his reach and give him one of his favorite toys to keep him occupied while you do the brushing. This can become a bad habit—while you're trying to do grooming, puppy is trying to mouth the brushes. Pick grooming implements appropriate for your dog's coat. A steel comb is very handy for removing the hair from the brush, and I always recommend the curved steel-tooth brushes to remove the hair going with the curve of the teeth, as opposed to against it. Taking the hair out against the bend of the teeth will eventually end up in unbending your brush and thereby making it less useful. I recommend that your dog be brushed on a daily basis if possible. It's very soothing to your dog, as well as stimulating to the dog's skin and hair. If daily sessions are not possible, at least once a week will suffice for medium-coated dogs. Long-coated dogs, such as Afghan Hounds and Maltese, will need more regular attention. I do not

"Aaron" being brushed with a curved toothed brush by trainer Francisco Gomez.

starting from the base of the neck back along the body. If your dog has feathering on his feet, brush up against the feathering, then down. Brush up and down on the chest, and when doing ears that have feathering, hold the leather of the ear in your hand to support the ear while you gently brush and stroke. Make it into an enjoyable experience.

recommend novice dog owners attempting to cut toenails since this can be risky. Teeth as well should be cleaned by your veterinarian. Grooming also enables you to see and feel your dog's body should there be something stuck in his fur and to check for some unusual lump or bump. Of course, if you detect any such growth, take him to your veterinarian as soon as possible.

When grooming your dog, make it a pleasant experience. Talk to your dog while you groom him,

SUPPLIES

You will find that owning a dog is very similar to bringing a new child into the family, partly suggested by the fact that you will need a variety of supplies for all of the puppy's needs and amenities. Pick an appropriate brush to suit the coat of your dog, for example: Long hair will require a slicker type of brush which has curved teeth, so that it can draw through the hair, clearing out matting and tangles. This type of brush is also very good at removing dead hair or dead undercoat from your dog. If your dog has short hair, I generally recommend a bristle brush because the dog's hair is close and short. Usage of a brush such as the one mentioned previously could actually scratch his skin. The short-haired dog, on the other hand, enjoys being brushed briskly with a bristle brush. This will not only stimulate the skin and remove the dead hair but it will also bring oil from the dog's hair into his coat.

NAILS

I generally recommend leaving nail clipping up to your local veterinarian. Dogs have a vein in each nail referred to as the quick. If your dog has clear nails you can generally see where this vein or quick ends. However, if a dog has dark or black nails, this becomes rather difficult. The danger lies in that if you cut into the quick itself your dog will bleed profusely, and although this is not fatal, the bleeding is sometimes very difficult to stop. Veterinarians are equipped for this type of emergency and have cauterizing instruments. Although dog nail clippers are commonly sold in most pet shops, I strongly recommend leaving this procedure to your vet. If by some chance or absolute necessity it does become necessary for you to clip your dog's nails, I recommend purchasing some coagulative or cauterizing powder, or a styptic stick or liquid, just in case you should cut into the dog's quick.

EARS

I recommend cleaning your dog's ears at least once a week. This can be easily done using cotton pads, such as women use to take off their makeup, and rubbing alcohol. Place a small amount of rubbing alcohol on the cotton pad and wipe the flap of the dog's ear. You will find that rubbing alcohol, being a universal solvent, will dissolve most waxes and dirts on your dog's ear and leave them clean and fresh. In regard to the canal of your dog's ear, we do not recommend trying to clean any deeper than you can possibly reach into with the first digit of your index finger. Should you see that there is dirt further down into the ear, we recommend taking the dog to your veterinarian. This way, these ears can be cleaned professionally without any danger of damaging your dog's eardrum.

TEETH

Do not overlook your dog's teeth when considering his general upkeep. Too many owners think their dogs' teeth will clean themselves. Dogs need chew toys and bones such as Nylabone® to help keep their teeth clean. Plaque develops on the dog's gums just like it does on that of humans. I recommend having your veterinarian clean your dog's teeth whenever you take him to the office for booster shots.

However, you too will begin to recognize that when your dog appears to have tartar, a yellowish brownish crust on the teeth, it is generally time to get the dog's teeth cleaned. Owners should brush their dogs' teeth once a week ideally. Your vet or pet shop will have suitable brushes and special toothpaste for your dog. Many dog people also use the Nylafloss®, a nylon rope device designed to clean between the dog's teeth. Do NOT use cotton ropes for dogs. The device can be played with by the owner and dog by the owner's gently tugging. Teeth are important to the dog for eating, protection, and of course the necessary chewing. It is the owner's responsibility to keep his dog from losing its teeth. Don't be passive in this regard or else your best friend may soon be toothless!

Brush your dog's teeth in an up and down motion.

BATHING

Baths should be given to the dog on a regular basis, generally when the dog is getting dirty or has a foul odor. Many excellent bathing solutions are available at pet shops. I recommend those that indicate that they will not burn your dog's eyes, and are gentle to your dog's hair. When bathing your dog, select an appropriate area. If you live in an apartment, I recommend

Francisco preparing to give "Aaron" a bath.

bathing your dog in the shower stall to avoid messing up the bathroom or other rooms of the house, since dogs do tend to shake quite a bit after they have been bathed. I would recommend getting the dog thoroughly wet, either with your shower hose or shower head, and then shutting the water; putting on an adequate amount of soap to foam up the dog's body quite thoroughly, avoiding eyes, of course; and then rinsing, starting with the head and working your way back so that the soap is removed from your dog's face and eye area immediately. After the

soap has been rinsed thoroughly from all parts of your dog, including his groin, stomach and chest areas, squeeze the hair with your hands to get as much water out as possible, then allow your dog to shake thoroughly in the shower before letting him out. Once the shaking has been completed, I recommend toweling your dog down with a big thick terry towel. If you live in a very cold climate or if the weather is very bad, you can simply let the dog stay in a warm room with a couple of towels on the floor. In situations where more rapid drying is required, you can use the same type of hair dryer you would use on your own hair. However, do keep the setting down and the speed low so that it doesn't frighten your dog.

DOG TOYS

Dogs enjoy playing with toys every bit as much as children do. With dogs, as with children, we have an obligation to make sure that the toys we supply to our dogs are safe. A type of toy that might be safe with one type of dog may very well not be safe with another. Dogs that have very sharp teeth, very strong jaws and use their mouths considerably should be given toys that are far more durable than those for a playful little puppy. There's a very large selection of toys available on the market. One of the product lines that we recommend quite regularly to our clients are the Nylabone® line of dog toys. They're extremely durable, virtually indestructible, and come in a variety of shapes, sizes and colors. There is a company that actually takes cow bones, demarrows them, then bakes and dries them so that you get a sterile dry animal bone in a package. This is a very good toy for dogs to teethe on, and it is also a source of calcium. In addition, this type of toy will be very durable, and you don't have to worry about the dog ingesting an excessive marrow, which at times can upset a dog's stomach. I think just using good commonsense will be the best recommendation I can give you on the selection of your dog's toys. They should be durable and easily cleaned and disinfected. The

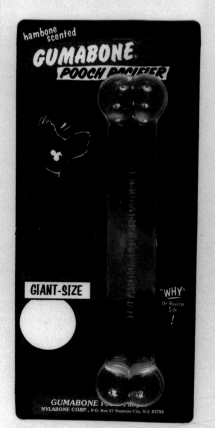

The Gumabone® by the makers of Nylabone® is scientifically proven to protect a dog's teeth. Although a number of manufacturers offer similar products, the Gumabone® and Nylabone® are the originals and the best.

Nylabone® can be boiled for sanitation purposes. Also, they should be a type that could not present itself as a danger to your dog. If you use these statements as your guidelines, you will have no trouble finding safe and durable toys for your dog.

HOUSING

Dogs, on the whole, enjoy having an area or place of their own. In its atavistic state, the pack would normally dwell in a cave, so it's not unusual to find that our domesticated pets still retain that recessive trait. These areas can vary from spacious brick dog runs to red wooden doghouses. In my time I have seen clients have doghouses built as replicas of their own homes, from cedar shakes to tile roofs. The dog's place can even be an area in a utility room with a large mat or basket, and the bedding can vary from cedar chips to stripped-up newspaper to an old piece of carpeting. However, no matter what you eventually use, I highly recommend that you assign your dog an area that he will learn to call his own. This will be a place for him to go to when he just feels like having some time out, possibly when he's not feeling too well, and also for those times when you need him out of the way. In addition, it is advisable to have a regular place for him to sleep, and this area can work quite well for that as well. Dogs are creatures of habit, and so once conditioned to this area, not only will your dog understand what you mean when you say, "Go to your place," but he will also learn to rely on this special area when he wishes to be alone.

YOUR DOG'S SPECIAL PLACE AND SANITATION

I recommend that doghouses be draft-free. I also recommend that the doghouse be raised off the ground approximately six to eight inches. This can be done easily with bricks or some type of wood foundation. The primary purpose of this is to keep the bottom of the doghouse from absorbing moisture and cold from the ground. Depending on the area you live in, these considerations will vary; however, regardless of the degree of moisture or coldness present, it is highly advisable for the doghouse to be raised. This will prevent the bottom of your dog's house from becoming cold as well

Chain- link day run with cement block dividing wall.

as from absorbing moisture, and thus protect your dog from developing rheumatism, arthritis or colds. The doghouse should be placed so that the doorway to it is directed away from any wind, and if you live in an area where it does get extremely cold in the wintertime, you might also consider putting some type of cut flap over the doorway to keep out some of the bitterness of the cold and wind. There are also companies that make electrically heated mats to be placed in doghouses for dogs that live in cold climates. These help keep the doghouse at a reasonable temperature, even during the coldest of days. The roof of the doghouse should be water-tight, obviously to prevent water from leaking in during rain or snow. And if at all possible, insulate the roof and house if you live in a cold climate. If your dog's special area is going to be indoors, any number of items can be used for a area or mat such as earlier described. The important thing to keep in mind once again is that the dog is not laying on a cold or concrete floor, so that his area won't be absorbing moisture or cold from the concrete. If you should elect to provide your dog with a bed, choose one that is sturdy. There are a number of different dog beds on the market, and I think the use of good commonsense can help you select one of a sturdy nature. If you are using indoor/outdoor carpeting as bedding material, this is easily cleaned with water and soap. If you are using some other kind of cotton or fabric type of material for the bedding, try to select something that is machine-washable so that it can be regularly sanitized. In addition, if your dog has a house which is outside in a dog run, in constructing the run, if at all possible, do it so that the dog run drains away from the doghouse. If at all possible, have a drain installed, so that when it does rain or snow the water will go down a drain away from your dog's house instead of puddling underneath it. In addition, the dog run too must be sanitized on a regular basis. Most pet shops carry various solutions that can be used for this purpose. However, something such as a normal household disinfectant can be used as well. Whatever product you do use, make sure you thoroughly rinse it from this surface after the cleaning and disinfecting process so that there is no residue left. If your dog run happens to be gravel, make sure the gravel is at least four to six inches deep. This way, when it rains, the water will drain down through the gravel into the ground, still leaving your dog with a reasonably dry surface. I do not recommend dirt or grass dog runs, because of sanitation and drainage difficulties. Regardless of how well you pick up stool from a grass or dirt run, residue will always remain behind, and when wet, moisture will tend to stay on the surface and puddle. Make sure that the children of the family understand that the dog's area is specifically his and that they don't violate the dog's privacy when he is in this area. Most dogs are extremely tolerant of children; however, even with this tolerance they need time alone for rest and sleep. It is for these reasons I strongly recommend that the children in the family as well as the other members learn to respect your dog's area as being his special place.

Although children will many times take the dog's toys to play with for their own—sometimes just out of interest, sometimes to tease—this is unfair to your dog. I also highly recommend that the dog's right to his toys as well as his place be considered with respect. In my many years of training dogs, I have found it much easier to train a dog to respect his family's limits and the children's property when those same respects are afforded the dog. I don't suggest that a dog has the same intelligence as a adult human being; however, I think they in many ways do have the same feelings. When we're teaching a puppy to respect the parameters of the family, the privacy of the family members and their property as well as the children's toys, we need to have a policy which is reasonably fair to the dog in return. As frustrating as it is for a young child to have a toy taken from him, it is equally as taunting and frustrating for a puppy.

Problem Solving

CAR SICKNESS

Occasionally we run into incidences of car sickness with puppies. Commonly the puppy has a queasy stomach when in motion in a car, boat, or airplane. This is usually attributed to disturbing the dog's center of balance. Make sure when working on a car sickness exercise that the puppy has not had anything to eat for at least five hours prior to practicing the exercise. This will minimize any chance of upsetting the pup's stomach.

The best way to deal with this issue is by placing the puppy in the car with you, in the driveway or parked on the street. Leave the windows open so that there is plenty of ventilation but not so wide open that the puppy can jump out. Take a magazine—make yourself comfortable. The idea is to relate to the puppy that it is safe and comfortable to be in the motionless vehicle. Make it fun for the pup and bring along a toy or two. The object is to get the puppy over the fear of being in the car. Repeat this exercise for approximately 20 minutes twice a day over a one-week period. Once this has been accomplished, we are ready to move on to the next step, which will be repeating the exercise and interjecting the radio, preferably playing soft quiet music; continue this exercise for another five days. At this point we will move on to the third step, which will be to put the puppy in the car, turn on the motor, and let the motor run for five or ten minutes. Then shut the motor off and sit another ten minutes in the car with the puppy. Continue this exercise for an additional week.

Now we are ready to take the puppy for a bit of a drive. The car should be driven slowly, so pick a quiet street where this can be done. Drive slowly for a short period of no more than 10 or 15 minutes, then park the car and sit with the puppy with the radio playing. At all times make sure there is plenty of ventilation in the car. Again, do not open the windows to a point where the puppy could possibly fall out or jump out. I would suggest, depending on the style of car that you have, that you restrict the puppy's movement by using a short chain leash so that the puppy can feel free to move about the back seat of your sedan or the bed of your station wagon. Never use a leash so long that the puppy can leap over the seat into your lap, or into other areas of the car where his presence could be dangerous. You will find following this process and increasing the length of the trips will effectively eliminate car sickness.

CAR SAFETY

If by some chance you have occasion to leave your dog in your car, either when out on an errand or in the course of travel, we very adamantly ask you to be aware of the fact that the temperature in a car can go from room temperature to an excess of 100 degrees in a matter of minutes, if the dog is parked in the sun. Dogs are very susceptible to heat prostration, and I recommend avoiding the situation as much as possible. When absolutely unavoidable, park the car in the shade and leave the windows open enough to keep air circulating throughout the car, which will keep the temperature down. I also recommend leaving some water in a pan for the dog in the car, so he can at least get a drink should he get thirsty. Make sure the windows are not open far enough for wandering

"I'm off for a drive."

Corina Kamer with friend "Murphy" in wading pool.

hands to come in or for your dog to squeeze out, and under all circumstances minimize the amount of time your dog will be left in the car.

When traveling with your dog, should the occasion arise where you have to leave your dog in a hotel room, I advise that you make the room as dog-proof as possible. That means removing anything that could be dangerous to the puppy or that might be something he could get into and destroy. Give your dog a few of his favorite toys; in addition, I find leaving on the television or radio for some distraction works quite well at keeping your dog company while you are out of the room. Here, too, I recommend minimizing the amount of time your dog will have to be in a strange environment unattended. Dogs are much the same as children, in that if they are left in a strange environment on their own they will often feel insecure or get into mischief.

SWIMMING POOL SAFETY

Since many dog owners nowadays have swimming pools at home, and/or have access to swimming pools, we feel it necessary to include some training for these people. It is very important to understand that to a puppy the surface of a pool often appears as a solid surface—this can be quite dangerous. Dogs naturally know how to swim; however, they do not know how to get out of swimming pools. The biggest danger with dogs who fall into the pool is that, in not knowing how to get out of the pool, they will continue to swim until they exhaust themselves, and unfortunately drown. That's why it is extremely critical that, if you have a swimming pool, your puppy learn at a young age where the steps are in your swimming pool. We accomplish this by the following: The equipment to be used will be your dog's slip chain and leather leash. Walk your puppy over to the edge of your pool where the steps are. (Put on a bathing suit, because we're gonna get a little wet here!) Take him out to the pool where the steps are and tell him to "Sit-Stay." You start off by walking down to the second step, telling your puppy, "Come," and reeling him in on the leash as we did initially in his "Come" exercise. If he is a bit reluctant, encourage

him to "Come" toward you until his feet are entirely in the water and he is standing on the step. Praise him briskly and make sure that he understands this is a game, not a discipline, and maybe splash a little water at him or wrestle a bit with him on the first step. If your puppy is aquatic and seems to enjoy this, go down to the next step, and the next step, bringing him down one step at a time until he swims a bit. Once he is swimming, go back to the steps, tell him, "Come," and lead him over to the steps by the leash until his feet are on the steps; back up out of the pool, telling him, "Come," until he is out with you. Praise him briskly, both physically and verbally, and let him know this is exactly what you wanted. As this lesson

Supervision of dogs and children is critical.

plan matriculates, practice this routine with your dog approximately 15 to 20 minutes each day. As your dog seems to comprehend where the steps are, play this game until he can be midway out in the pool, and you can go back to the the puppy get into the water, accept and tolerate it, and then to call him out of the water so that he learns where the steps are. If you find that you have a dog that does not particularly care for the water, continue this

"Out I come."

steps and say "Come" and your puppy can swim back to you and get out of the pool. This will assure you that he has developed the ability to know where the steps are as well as the physical strength to swim on a regular basis and to get himself out of the pool.

If you have a dog that seems to be shy of the water, this exercise should be continued in shorter periods of time. Remember the basic goal is to have

exercise until it is apparent to you that your dog from midway in the pool can swim back to the steps when you call him and get out of the pool. The object here is not necessarily to have a puppy fall in love with swimming but rather that he knows where the steps are and can get out of the pool.

JUMPING
Jumping is one of the

more typical problems that we're confronted with when training young puppies. This usually comes from the fact that puppies are very glad to see you when you come home and are easily excited. The easiest way to deal with this problem is a direct correction as follows: Dogs have peripheral vision, which means they see in the span of a fan. When a puppy jumps up, his line of sight is above your knee. When your puppy jumps on you, bump him softly with your knee without any verbal correction. Puppies, much the same as children, will stop something more quickly when it is inconvenient to them than if they think that they have found some way of pushing mommy or daddy's buttons. The short direct bump will normally result in dropping your puppy

backwards to his side. When the puppy rights himself, praise him briskly, then tap your thighs and encourage the dog to come back and jump on you again. Should the puppy take this cue, once again without verbal correction bump the puppy off and back with your knee. The purpose of utilizing this form of correction is so that, regardless if it were a child or a friend who in all innocence taps his thighs and encourages the pup to jump up toward him, the puppy will run up still wagging his tail, happy

Bumping a jumping puppy "Off."

and bright; but instead of jumping on you or your guests, soiling clothes, scratching legs, possibly grabbing at clothes with his teeth or paws, the puppy will tend to stay close, waiting for the praise and affection without the unwanted jumping up.

Jumping On Furniture

Jumping on furniture is another more common problem that we deal with daily with our puppy friends. The following is the most expedient way to deal with this issue. Bring your puppy into a room on leash and collar as a part of his normal lesson, preceding it or following it. Walk him toward the couch or chairs in the room, tap the top of the pillows on the chairs and say, "No!" Walk around the room to any piece of furniture that you do not want your puppy going up on, and rather than waiting till the puppy jumps up on it to reprimand him, begin orienting the dog to the house by walking the dog through the house, and tapping the various objects you do not want the puppy near or on and sternly telling him, "No!" Now should you find that you have a precocious little guy, who when loose in the house comes running up to you and attempts to jump up on a couch or pillow, with the broad side of your hand simply push the puppy back and say, "No! Off! Bad dog!" and then ignore him. If the puppy tries to come back up again, repeat the exercise, saying, "No! Off!" He'll flop over on his side. Then, totally ignore him. He will quickly learn that this is not something you want and will cease the behavior.

"No" while pointing to object on to which the dog is not to jump.

If you should be walking through a room and see your dog up on a piece of furniture, briskly walk over to the dog, take him by his collar, pull him off the couch and say, "No! Bad dog!" Leave him in that room again and observe him peripherally by walking past the door. Should he even consider going back on, run into the room, slap the top of the pillow, and in a stern tone of voice again say, "No! Bad dog!"

Fence Jumping

Fence jumping is another common problem with dogs. If you find that you have a dog that jumps fences, the following technique works quite effectively. Have a friend wait on the far side of the fence where your dog cannot see him. Create the atmosphere—one of the key issues to keep in mind is that many of the problems require "baiting." I wish to point out that this is not cruel in any way; in fact, it is much more humane than allowing the dog to go on with negative activity, which may result in harm and his alienation from the family. By creating the baited situation you can, when you have the time, work on these negative behaviors, as opposed to

Leandra Kamer telling "T.J." "No, bad dog. Off!" as she pulls him off a bench he should not be on. She is pulling him by the collar he is wearing.

hearing from the neighbors or friends that your dog is misbehaving when you're not home. Have a friend wait on a far side of the fence, hidden in a bush or behind a tree, with a large straw broom. Then create the situation which baits your dog to jump, whether it's leaving him out in the yard by himself, his hearing your car drive off, a dog barking down the street, etc. Let me point out that there is no good reason for your dog to be jumping the fence. When the dog appears to be jumping up on the fence, and his front feet hit the top of the fence or wall, have your friend dash out and tap your dog firmly on the feet with the straw broom, shouting, "Bad dog! Bad dog, no!" The person should not mention the dog's name, and he should be a stranger to the dog, so that the dog will think that there's an enemy on the other side of the wall waiting for him to come back. This will normally abort the jumping process. If you have a dog that jumps excessively, especially when you're gone, and you cannot work on this issue in a controlled manner such as described above, we will offer an alternative.

Purchase a dowel appropriate to the size of your dog, one inch in diameter for large dogs, one-half inch for medium-size dogs, one-fourth inch for small dogs. Cut a length of this dowel to the width of your dog plus two inches. In the center of this dowel place an eye screw, then cut a piece of parachute cord just long enough to hang from the ring in your dog's collar to the eye bolt in the dowel. Tie this cord to the eye bolt in such a manner that when connected to your dog's collar ring, it will hang just above his knees. This will allow your dog to run around the yard freely when you're not there to control him, and yet should he attempt to jump the fence, the dowel will pop up under his chin, and then down on his knees; this quickly will inhibit him from

Waiting with broom poised for wall jumping dog correction.

Parachute cord and snap lock used to correct bolting dog.

wanting to jump. However, this does not replace the need for you to work with your dog in the controlled manner described above.

issue. The most direct way of dealing with this is to have your puppy on a long leash or line of some very

DASHING OUT OF DOORS

Some puppies, during their early stages of their training, see an open door and are very tempted to dash out. Of course, this can be quite dangerous and has to be immediately eliminated as an

Trainer Carol Willman correcting a dashing pup. Let dog reach end of leash before pulling back. Then walk in opposite direction while saying "Heel."

strong cord, such as parachute cord. This is very lightweight and will not give your puppy the sense of having a training leash on. Tie the end of the parachute cord to the slip chain, or purchase a little snap lock to be tied from the end of the parachute cord to the slip chain. Allow the front door to be opened and hold the end of the parachute cord tied in a loop in your hand. If the puppy is prone to bolting, we will bait the situation by creating an atmosphere in which your puppy will be tempted to bolt. Create this atmosphere by allowing the dog to bolt and run out to the end of the leash. When your puppy hits the end of the leash, of course he will get a sudden jolt; now say in a loud, firm, corrective tone of voice, "No! Bad dog!" Reel in the leash briskly and bring your dog back to your side in a "Sit-Stay" position. Walk your dog around to distract him from the initial cause of the problem, namely the open doorway or gate, bring him back to the area and once again bait him with this technique.

CHEWING

Chewing can be a problem with your puppy. Dogs chew objects for a variety of reasons. As a smart owner you must realize that the pup needs to chew to develop its jaw, to bring in new teeth, to keep his teeth clean and to relieve his many adolescent tensions and boredom. After puppyhood, the dog will chew less but will never stop chewing entirely. An owner's goal is to direct the puppy's chewing energies towards positive results. Many products have been designed for the sake of chewing: rawhide chews, nylon bones, polyurethane toys, and many others. While many professionals are not content with rawhide, the nylon bone, particularly the Nylabone®, and the polyurethane toys namely Gumabone®, prove safe and especially useful in guiding the pup's chewing instinct. If the dog is provided with a number of these bones and toys, he will understand that these are acceptable chew objects and begin to regard these objects as his own. If however the dog persists on chewing the wrong objects (e.g., leather boots, furniture legs, door frames, etc.), you must take definite action to correct this behavior.

If you should catch your puppy chewing, immediately run over to him and sternly tell him he's a "Bad dog!" Point to the object he was chewing, slap it (the object, not the dog) with your hand, and making a loud noise say, of the house. We want your puppy to understand that when he is taken to this area, it is for a

Carol Willman preparing to correct a pulling dog.

"Bad dog!" Take your dog outside to an area we shall call the reprimand or correction area. This should be an isolated area, such as a quiet side of the house or backyard where you have a small pen for the dog so he can spend some time alone. This area should only be used for corrections, not at times when you need the dog out correction. If you do not have a fenced area appropriate for this application, you may buy yourself a four-to-six- foot chain leash, which can be fixed to any tree or fence post so that it is long enough for your puppy to sit or walk around comfortably, but short enough so that your puppy cannot lie down and take a nap. Dogs are very patient by nature. When you have shown your puppy something he has done incorrectly and he should persist in doing wrong after you have told him not to, take him to the isolation area. Using his leather collar (not a slip chain), tie him to this area and let him sit there for approximately 15 minutes to half an hour. Puppies are very patient, and we tend to concern ourselves when we have to reprimand our puppies. Start with a 15-minute period, which should be adequate to have your puppy understand that you're angry with him. When you return after the 15-minute period, walk your puppy back to the item he chewed on, the thing he did wrong, show it to him once again, slap it, tell him he's a bad dog and turn him loose in that area. Observe him periodically from a distance and see if he is tempted to go back to the article. If he does so right away, go up to him briskly, slap it again, take him back to the reprimand area, and leave him there for another 15 minutes to half an hour. One of the issues we are confronted with is that most owners will leave a dog for too short a period of time. Fifteen minutes is not an unreasonable period of time to isolate a dog for having been bad. Do not reduce this period of time, as it will not be effective.

DIGGING

Dogs dig for various reasons; sometimes they dig because they smell or sense rodents or gophers, other times because they sense something decaying underground. A third reason for digging is that many times dogs carry items away to bury, such as bones or toys, for the purpose of returning later to recover the items. This is a residue of a survival instinct from their atavistic state. However, this does not make it acceptable in your lovely garden. Determine first that the cause of the digging is not rodents or gophers, and if it is, eliminate the rodents.

Should you find that you have a digging puppy, we will proceed as follows: First show the puppy the area that he dug; tell him that he is a bad dog, scolding him with a stern tone of voice; and take him to the reprimand area, leaving him there for approximately 15 minutes. During this process, fill in the hole, pack it down firmly, and then sprinkle "moth crystals" (not mothballs) on the area. Dogs do not like the scent of moth crystals. After the 15-minute period of isolation, take your puppy back to the area where he was digging. He will instinctively start to smell the area out of curiosity; once he gets a nose full of the odor, he will normally be deterred from returning to that area.

Should you find for some reason that your puppy is not bothered by moth crystals (which happens rarely), another step that might be taken would be to set mousetraps. Fill in the hole about 90%, then put in the set mousetraps covered by newspapers and top it off by covering it with dirt. When your puppy returns to this area to dig, the traps will be set off harmlessly under the newspapers and startle your dog. He will run away, effectively deterred from returning to this area. In addition, your puppy gets to know the

reprimand area quite well as a punishment for any activity he should not be doing. So this method can be used along with the mousetraps.

NUISANCE BARKING

Barking can be caused by a number of stimulants. For instance, strange noises out on the street, strange animals coming up to your property perimeters, your dog's natural protectiveness, your dog noisily wanting to come into the house. The first thing we need to do is to determine the cause of the barking. If it is the dog's instinct to be protective because some strange person or animal

The reprimand area should allow the dog to sit or stand—not lie down. Be sure that the area is shaded and that water is provided.

is close to your property, try to deal with eliminating or reducing this type of situation in itself. In today's environment, we don't want to discourage your dog from being naturally protective. If we find we have a nuisance barker, such as a dog who barks because he wants to come in, wants to go out, or needs something else, we would eliminate this problem as follows: Take an empty soda can and fill it with about 15 or 20 coins, and tape the hole closed. This is known as a "shaker can." Should you find your dog barking unnecessarily when he is outside, open the door suddenly and shout, "No! No, bad dog" and throw the shaker can at the ground in front of him. This will startle your dog, and, not enjoying the experience, he will quickly stop the behavior. The startling effect of the shaker can will rather perplex him as to how it occurred. At this point in time, using your correcting tone of voice, firmly say, "No! Bad dog!" close the door, and repeat the baiting process after a ten-minute wait. In addition to the shaker can, we have found that blowing a loud whistle also effectively startles your dog into listening to your spoken command.

Remember, ascertain what the stimulus is that makes your dog bark so that you can duplicate it, and bait him so that you can, during the time available, catch him and correct him in a controlled manner—as opposed to having to stay home from work in order to accomplish this goal.

A loud whistle kept handy is a good way to get your dog's attention before saying "No" or "Bad dog" for a negative behavior.

Housebreaking

Using the basic premise of my praise technique (show the dog how to do something, repeat lesson and praise him for being right), you will find that housebreaking is relatively simple. If the following procedure is implemented properly, it will not be a tremendous chore to you or confusing to your dog. Remember, we are going to show the puppy how to be right and praise him for this, rather than scold and confuse him for being wrong.

We're going to take advantage of our knowledge of dogs and their natural instincts: normal dogs keep their sleeping quarters clean and will not dirty their beds unless physically ill. The first step in our process will be to purchase a fully enclosed "puppy home" (such as a traveling crate). Buy a size appropriate to your dog's size and needs. Dogs generally love having their own place of security, as well as a "home away from home" for travel. Putting a dog in a crate is by no means cruel. Every top-winning show dog in the world spends at least 25%

of his life in a cage or crate. Having his own place or den relates back to a dog's atavistic heritage, in which wild dogs slept in caves for protection and security. In addition, once your dog has completed this aspect of his training, the crate door can be left open and you will find your dog going in and out of his crate when he's tired or needing privacy. Locate the crate in a draft-free area, and away from heat or air conditioning vents. Next we need to establish the appropriate schedule.

DAILY SCHEDULE

1. Bedtime: Take the puppy outside to the area you wish him to use as his bathroom, and give him the opportunity to exercise. Always use the same door to take your dog out so that he will learn which door to go through when he needs to relieve himself. If he has relieved himself in a certain spot in the yard, take him back to the same spot. If you have a small fenced-in area, let him run loose. If he is to be on-leash, don't choke him. Use a leather collar for exercise or a properly

Four Paws
Wee-Wee
Pads are
scientifically
treated to
attract puppies
when nature
calls. The
plastic lining
prevents
damage to
floors and
carpets.

fitting training collar on the "inactive" (non-closing) ring. We don't wish to do anything to deter the dog from his appointed task. It might be particularly wise if you have a small breed and you want to paper-train the puppy to also purchase an exercise pen. This can be used outside in the chosen area with the puppy loose, or use it indoors with plenty of newspaper. Always keep a small piece of "soiled" paper to put on the fresh papers, as dogs do everything by scent. When he relieves himself, praise your dog briskly and let him know how proud you are of him. Keep praising him, take him inside at once and put him in "the crate" for the evening.

2. Morning: First thing— pick him up and take him outside (or put him in his exercise pen with the paper). Remember! The exercise pen can also be used outside with paper. He's tried to be clean all night, so hurry and he will do his "business" in a rush. Now, bring him in and give him freedom in a confined area, like the kitchen with the door blocked (a children's safety gate works well and is easily available) or the playroom, but only if you are going to be supervising him.

3. Feeding: After you have eaten breakfast and done your first morning chores, feed him his food. The food should be left down as long as the puppy

Puppy out on leash. It is necessary to allow the puppy to go outside after every meal.

continuously eats. Once the puppy stops and walks away, the food and water should be picked up. He's had freedom up to this point, but after he eats, take him outside to the chosen area or put him in the exercise pen. After he has "exercised" and you have seen that he has relieved himself, bring him inside and put him in his crate. Then water can be offered. The meals should be offered in the morning, noon and evening consistently as long as the puppy continues to eat.

4. Noon: Take him out of the crate, and put him outside or in the exercise pen until you have seen he has relieved himself.

5. Bring him in after he eliminates, and once again, give him the confined freedom with you for one or two hours. If your puppy takes three meals a day, this would be the time to feed him his lunch. Afterwards, repeat steps three and four.

6. Dinner time: (4:00–5:00 pm) Take him out of the crate for another opportunity to relieve himself in the selected area. Bring him in for confined freedom with supervision while you prepare your dinner and his. After you eat, feed the puppy; then, just as soon as he finishes, take him outside to the designated area. Naturally, you can feed him before you eat as long as you have the time to follow the exercising procedure, but DO NOT feed him later than 6:00 pm!

7. After dinner: Allow him controlled and confined freedom. Allow him to be with you in the kitchen or playroom until approximately 8:00 pm. Then, he should again be taken to the outside area or put in the pen. Just before you retire, go through the bedtime routine (1).

If you continue this routine for approximately two weeks, you will find that the pattern has been established. Now you can start to check on his learning by allowing him a little more freedom from his crate. Incidentally, when the puppy is out of the crate, the door is always left open in case he wants to go back in. The extended freedom is still only in the confined area, just as in the morning. If he is good, the next day allow confined and controlled freedom in the afternoon as well. Do not test your puppy all night until this pattern has been repeated for at least two weeks. Now it is time to begin limited introduction to the other rooms of the home, but only when you are with the puppy and when your attention is on him. In addition, have your puppy on-leash while you're watching television (we find many people get absorbed in their programs and don't pay proper attention to the puppy during this crucial training time). IMPORTANT: During these periods of freedom, be sensitive to any whining or attempts to go to the door, as well as to any loss of interest in you or a toy, or any purposeful circling around. If any of these signals appear, immediately take your puppy to the area or pen. If by some chance your puppy has an "accident," let him know by your voice and expression that you are angry with this and that he is bad, and put him outside in the designated area or in the pen. In order to do this correctly, you must catch the dog in the act or very shortly thereafter. *You* can then correct him for something he's done. You can *not* correct him for something he has done several hours earlier, since their association with things is very limited. Should the puppy have several accidents or soil his bed, check the following:

• Worms—have the veterinarian examine the stool sample.

• Diet—don't vary your puppy's diet. Follow the veterinarian's recommendations as to food products to be used and number of meals per day.

• Water—only give water with food while you are housebreaking. Do not leave water or uneaten food around while teaching clean habits.

• Clean any "accident" area thoroughly with commercial spot and odor disinfectant removers. Remember, his nose gives him the idea to "go."

Feed on a regulated schedule, and leave the food and water down as long as your dog continues to eat. When he walks away, it is time to pick up both water and food. This inhibits snacking, and also unnecessary bowel movements and urination throughout the day. During freedom periods, you may walk or train your dog. This helps to cement a closer relationship between you, as well as increasing your dog's composure.

Have your puppy wear a roll leather collar when not undergoing formal lessons on his slip chain and leash. This will give you a "handle" to hold onto him when necessary during correction exercises.

When housebreaking your puppy, make sure to pick up the puppy and carry him outside to the elimination area whenever he wakes up from a nap. Young puppies tend not to have very strong control over their bowels and bladder, and if they have been sleeping and have to eliminate, they may just drip on their way out the door. To avoid this unnecessary cleanup, I recommend carrying your dog out to the "potty" spot, and rewarding your puppy with physical and verbal praise after he eliminates.

Try to be observant of your dog's bathroom habits. For example, my wife and I have recently obtained a new German Shepherd puppy, and we've noticed that she likes to relieve herself not only after her naps but also first thing in the morning, after each of her meals, and before bed. We turn those periods into positive learning experiences by taking her to the same area, and rewarding her for eliminating with physical and verbal praise. This prevents her inadvertently eliminating in the house and requiring a reprimand. If by some chance you don't have her pattern down and the puppy does start to eliminate in the house, quickly pick the puppy up, saying, "No, Bad," in a medium tone of voice (not a severe reprimand tone of voice), and take the puppy to the spot that you want the dog to relieve in. Allow the dog a little extra time to relieve himself, since the puppy was somewhat startled from this maneuver and had already begun to eliminate. Should you find that your dog has completed relieving himself in some area of the house, take him to it, show it to him, and in a severe tone of voice say, "BAD, BAD!! NO, NO!!" Then take the puppy to the area you wish the puppy to relieve himself in and leave the puppy there alone for at least a half hour. In this manner, your puppy will understand the difference between a minor correction and a reprimand of more severity.

Showing Your Dog

For those of you who become totally enraptured with your new pet and are looking for an interesting and rewarding hobby, showing your dog should be seriously considered. The American Kennel Club sponsors dog shows throughout the year all over the United States. The dogs are exhibited by breed and all compete within a designated group. There is a Sporting Group, a Hound Group, a Working Group, a Terrier Group, a Toy Group, a Non-sporting Group and a Herding Group. In these shows, only registered purebred dogs are exhibited.

There are a number of classes within each breed being exhibited that you may choose to enter your dog in, depending on age and experience. The breed classes are broken down by age and sex. Within each breed you will find a number of classifications. Puppies are typically exhibited in either the 6–9 months class or the 9–12 months class. Once your dog is over a year of age, you may choose to exhibit your dog in either the novice class, bred by exhibitor class, or open class. There is also an American-bred class. The two puppy classes are fairly self-explanatory. They are, as their respective titles indicated, for puppies between six to nine months of age and for puppies nine to twelve months of age. The novice class is generally for dogs that are new to the show ring and have little experience. Bred by exhibitor class is reserved for dogs that are being shown by the people who bred the dogs. American-bred class is reserved for dogs bred in the United States out of American breeding lines. Open is generally the class one would elect to put his dog in if the dog is reasonably mature and has some ring experience. In each class, dogs compete against other dogs that have been entered into that class, and a winner first through fourth will be selected within each class. The same classifications are available in male dogs, which are referred to as dogs, and female dogs, which are referred to as bitches.

Once a first place winner has been selected in each

of the six classes, the six winning male dogs will compete against each other for the winners dog ribbon and the reserve winners dog ribbon. The female dogs exhibited in the same six classes will have their first place winners come back into the ring to compete for the winners bitch ribbon and the reserve winners bitch ribbon.

Points are awarded at each dog show, and a schedule of the points available at each dog show can be found in the dog show catalogue, which is available at each respective dog show. The points can vary from one to five at an individual dog show, since the allotment of points are based upon the number of dogs within a given breed, both dogs and bitches, being exhibited that day. The points awarded will either be one point or two points, which is considered a minor, or three to five points, which is considered a major. Once a winners dog and a winners bitch has been selected, they will come back into the ring, along with any AKC champions entered in the breed. These dogs will then compete for a best of breed, a best of opposite sex, and a best of winners. The best of winners is

chosen from the winners dog and winners bitch. If the number of points available the day of the show based on entries is greater for the opposite sex of your breed and your dog or bitch has won best of winners, you will be awarded the greater number of points in lieu of the points available from the class your dog or bitch won in.

To have your dog become an AKC champion, your dog or bitch must accrue a total of 15 points over a number of shows. The 15 points must consist of at least two major wins, meaning that your dog or bitch competed in a dog show and the number of dogs and bitches present that day resulted in an award of three, four, or five points. Other than the two majors, the balance of the points can be comprised of wins and any number of points over a period of time.

Once a best of breed has been selected for your breed for the day, the winner of the best of breed competition will compete later in the day against the best of breed winners from the Group. The winner of the Group, called Group First, competes aginst the six other Group winners. The winner of that

Leandra Kamer teaching the eight-week-old "Buck" to "Stack" for show.

competition is referred to as the best in show.

Each breed has a standard recognized by the American Kennel Club, which is the governing body of the dog show world in the United States. Those standards are available from the American Kennel Club, and basically explain what a "perfect" example of your breed should be; areas such as structure, quality of coat, size, temperament, overall appearance, balance, angulation, and gait all come into play. As a rule, the dogs or bitches in any given class are lined up by their handlers, are reviewed for balance and expression then are gaited around the ring, giving the judge an opportunity to view the various entries based on fluidity of movement, and finally to examine each individually.

PREPARING FOR THE SHOW

To prepare your dog for conformation trials, we recommend familiarizing your dog with the procedures that he will be exposed to at the dog shows. This is best accomplished by taking your dog to dog shows and dog matches on a regular basis. It helps familiarize your dog with the environment, the tumult,

and the procedures which take place at the shows. Fun matches are held regularly throughout the United States and can be generally found either by calling your breed specialty club or through local newspapers. These are matches that are held periodically on the weekends, in which dogs get to compete against each other simply for fun. Ribbons are generally awarded, as are trophies, but points are not. American Kennel Club points are only awarded at AKC-sanctioned shows. At the AKC shows as well, ribbons and trophies are awarded.

We recommend beginning to train a show dog as young as three or four months of age, and it should be done in a play-type atmosphere. The show dog as well should undergo thorough on- and off-leash obedience training. Since show dogs must always stand by your side throughout show competition, the deletion of the "Automatic Sit" is highly recommended. Another option that you might wish to explore if your intent is to show your dog in both obedience and conformation trials is to proceed normally with the obedience training; however, make sure that when you are in a conformation trial and are coming to a stop, that you verbally tell your dog to "Stand." If you have effectively completed the "Standing" exercise of our obedience course, you will find that giving your dog this command when automatic "Sit" with a verbally commanded "Stand" periodically as you practice your various heeling exercises. We now have a puppy that is obedience-trained on- and off-leash, and also understands that he is to "Stand" when you come to a halt, unless you've chosen the option of simply deleting the

Demonstrating stacking of a dog for examination by a dog show judge.

you stop will tell your dog to remain in the "Standing" position. This exercise can be integrated with the normal obedience course by alternating the "Automatic Sit." The latter is recommended if your intention is to only show in conformation trials, the former is recommended if your intent is to show in both conformation and obedience trials.

STACKING

Stacking is training your dog to hold a "standing show position" so that in a conformation trial a judge can not only look at your dog but also examine your dog with his hands.

This is the position in which your dog is standing squarely by your side, with his front feet parallel to each other and his rear legs properly angulated behind him, putting his hock 90 degrees to the ground, and standing squarely. This exercise needs to be practiced over short periods of time so that your puppy's patience and tolerance of remaining in this position slowly grow. I recommend practicing this exercise not more than 12 to 15 minutes per session, two to three times per day, during the period of initial training. Once your dog has mastered this "Stand-Stack" position, I recommend practicing it once or twice a day in your dog's daily practice and show routine. I also recommend beginning a regiment of daily running. With young puppies, this daily trotting or jogging exercise should be done on soft surfaces, such as

grass or dirt, and should be for lengths of no more than approximately 50 yards per run. At this young age, your puppy is still growing. His bones and joints are soft and his ligaments and tendons are still maturing, and we don't want to overstress the puppy. As your dog reaches maturity and has practiced this exercise for several months, his ability and endurance will increase. The systematic running exercises will be firming up your dog, developing your dog's muscle tone and endurance, so that when he's ultimately being shown he will have the endurance to go through the multiple running exercises and stacking positions necessary at a dog show. I cannot stress too strongly that this should be done in a very happy and lighthearted manner, so that your dog enjoys this procedure and will ultimately show as a very happy, outgoing dog. Many times, owners in their zeal will overpractice with the dog, and although this may result in the dog mastering the exercise, the resulting crankiness can be points off at a dog show.

We can begin training the dog for stacking as a

part of obedience training. This would be done as follows: once you have your dog trained to heel on a leash, as you come to a stop tell him, "Stand." Since he already knows the word "Stand" he will remain standing. Then fold the leash over into your hand so that you are loosely holding the choke chain behind your dog's ears, and reach over and place his left front leg squarely under his shoulder. Switching hands and placing the left hand under the leash will free your right hand to place the right front leg parallel to the left front leg, showing the width of the dog's chest. Reach over the rear and place the left rear leg in back of the dog's tail, so that the hock is 90 degrees to the ground. Reach over with the left hand to the right rear leg and place the right rear leg parallel to the left rear leg, giving your dog reasonable width. You can then switch hands on the leash and hold your dog in this position to be examined. When you wish your dog to look especially alert, you may use something which we call "bait." This may be anything from your dog's favorite toy to a piece of cookie or boiled liver. The object is to have something that will excite your dog into an alert stacked position, ears up and alert, but not so excited that he breaks the stacked position and has to be replaced. When you heel with your dog, you can also practice moving with him in large counter-clockwise circles as well as straight-lined directions. Both these movements will be commonly used in conformation trials so that the judge can gauge your dog's gait and structure. When you gait with your dog, practice trotting, both at a normal gait and slowed down to where you can reasonably stop with your dog's feet somewhat forming the "Stacked" stance. I have seen many dogs that can literally be walked into a stack, and require very little, if any, assistance in completing the proper positioning. As part of this examination, a judge will want to check your dog's teeth as well, so you must get your dog used to his lips being rolled back and his teeth being exposed. This should be done not only by yourself but also by family members and friends, so that your dog will get used to this procedure and accept it easily. Also, the judge will be running his hands over your dog's body, feeling his structure and bones. This too should be practiced by having friends and family run their hands over the dog's body after he has been trained to accept a "Stack" position. Do not attempt the physical examination until the "Stack" exercise has been mastered first. Your dog should easily be able to hold a "Stack" for at least a minute or two before you attempt the physical examining. In the case of male dogs, please be advised that judges must check to see that your dog has both testicles descended. This is a dog show requirement. Needless to say, some practice must be put into this exercise as well so that your dog will not be particularly shy when examined in this manner.

BAITING

Many times at a dog show your dog will be distracted by any number of activities going on around him. I highly recommend finding some toy that your dog really gets excited over and using it as "bait." This item will be carried in a pocket on your right side, and at the moment of truth, once your dog has been "Stacked," you will take out this item and show it

to your dog to alert him. Caution must be taken in practicing with this item; first of all, don't overdo it, because your dog may become bored with the item and force you to seek a new one. Second of all, don't let the dog get so excited that he breaks the "Stack" position to get to the toy. A delicate point of balance must be achieved. Your dog must know that you will display the toy to him but that he must maintain the "Stack" position. However, once he and you have accomplished this procedure, he should be allowed to play with the toy for a brief period of time. Afterwards, take the toy and place it back in your pocket. Having a dog conditioned to respond to his favorite small toy as "bait" has enabled many a dog to become a champion.

Dog shows can have hundreds of entries and exhibitors, as well as hundreds, if not thousands of spectators. For this reason, I generally recommend investing in a portable puppy pen. These are available in varying heights and sizes. I advise buying one in your dog's appropriate overall size specifications at full growth. In addition, I would recommend buying a tarp

"Baiting" after "Stacking."

for the top of this portable pen. Many dog shows take place in open sunny areas, and the tarp will be useful in providing shade for you and your dog should you decide to join him "in his pen." (I must say I've done it many times myself.) I also recommend purchasing a three- or four-gallon water bucket so that there is plenty of water available. Many times it has to be hauled from an area far away from where you have set up your dog pen. These three items, and also some form of dolly or cart with wheels to haul these items around, are what I consider essentials when going to dog shows on a regular basis. I also recommend taking along some of your dog's food, or snacks such as dog biscuits, so that as the day wears on, should your dog become hungry you'll have some familiar food available. When traveling out of your area to dog shows, I have always found it advisable to take either bottled water or tapwater from home. Many times, different areas have different qualities to the water, and I have found that a dog's digestive systems can be quite sensitive to any change in water or food, especially when he's been traveling.

OBEDIENCE TRIALS

Obedience trials, I feel, are more complicated and try the proficiency of both man and dog quite a bit more than that of a conformation trial. Obedience classes are broken down by novice, which is also referred to as Companion Dog (CD); open, also referred to as Companion Dog Excellent (CDX); Utility, also known as Utility Dog (UD); and Tracking Dog (TD). The novice class comprises primarily of: heeling on-leash; standing for examination; heeling off-leash; a come exercise which is called a recall; a long sit; and a long down. This is a total of six exercises, and your dog will be graded on a point scale for his proficiency in each. Open work consists of seven exercises: heeling off-leash; dropping an article as you heel your dog, and then sending your dog back to retrieve it; your dog's ability to retrieve over a high jump; a broad jump followed by a long sit; and a long down exercise. Utility work consists of: a hand signal exercise; two scent discrimination exercises; a retrieving exercise, in which you must direct the retrieve to a specific direction and item; jumping over hurdles on command; and a group examination. There is a possibility for your dog to become a Companion Dog (CD) after he has achieved a score of 170 out of 200 at three consecutive shows, each win being considered a "leg." He must also achieve a score of 50% or better in each exercise. The scoring system is the same in each class of obedience trial. When your dog has become a utility dog, he can then collect points toward an obedience trial championship. To become an Obedience Trial Champion, your dog must win 100 points, including at least one first place in a utility competition against three other dogs; at least one first place in open, in competition against six other dogs; and one other first place win in either of these competitions. Each of these wins must be under a different judge. I recommend obedience trial competition only to those people with a great deal of time to dedicate to the daily practice and routine. The skill of dogs competing in obedience trials is quite high these days, and as in most performing arts, daily practice is essential to maintain a high degree of proficiency between you and your dog. When you enter the obedience trial ring, the exhibition is of your dog's capabilities at their peak. This can be a very rewarding experience, but it also requires a great deal of time, patience and dedication.

FIELD TRIALS

Field trials are expressly designed to evaluate your dog's ability to perform its primary function. They are designed for hunting breeds, of which there are four classifications: Hounds, Pointers, Retrievers, and Spaniels. Hounds are expected to trail and pursue rabbits, either in pairs or packs. Pointers are evaluated on their ability to aid the hunter by scenting the presence of a game bird, pointing to its location, and then on command flushing the same. Retrievers are measured on their ability to retrieve the game shot by their handler. Spaniels are graded on their ability to search out and detect other game, to flush the bird on command, and to retrieve same when ordered to do so, whether it be on land or water.

JUNIOR SHOWMANSHIP

For those of you with children, an interesting note is that there is also a Junior Showmanship class. This class is

Dalmatians have been used successfully in obedience trials.

Irish Water Spaniel practicing for obedience trial.

available to children 10-16. The children are judged on their skill and ability to handle their dogs, and the dogs entered must be AKC-registered, showable breeds, meaning breeds that can be shown in either conformation or obedience trials. The judging is heavily weighted towards the proficiency of the child to handle the dog, as opposed to the quality or the performance of the dog. Needless to say, a dog that performs well coupled with a handler that performs well is the ideal.

Regardless of which class of competition you select, you will find this to be a very rewarding and exciting sport. Good luck!

A Gallery of Kamer Students

"Kelly" ready on or off lead.

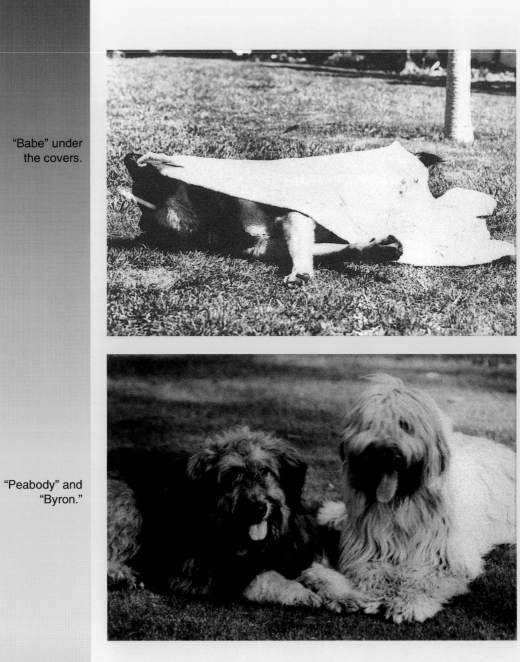

"Babe" under the covers.

"Peabody" and "Byron."

"Bongo" fetching the *L.A. Times.*

Author Michael Kamer placing at AKC dog show with Champion Scyldocga Brittania.

Michael Kamer and his champion Mastiff.

Top right: Bobby Womack and German Shepherd "Duchess." **Top left:** Donald Byrd and "Forte." **Bottom:** Patrick and Lisa Swazey with "Derek."

Sylvester Stallone and "Sheba."

Tina Turner
and "Sam."

Rod Stewart
and Britt
Eckland with
"Saba" and
puppy.

Rod Stewart
with two Irish
Setters.

John Frankenheimer and author Michael Kamer with "Matilda."

John Frankenheimer and German Shepherd "Matilda."

Michael Kamer
and "Macho."

Below: The
author kissed
by "Timber."
Below right:
Daniel Melnick
and "Joka."

Al Jarreau and "Pal."

Top left: Willie Aames and "Schultz." **Top right:** Gale Strom and "Drummer." **Right:** Ollie Brown and "Vuitton."

Sonny and Cher with "Brutus."

Bobbie and
Regina
Womack with
"Warrior."

Prince Salmen
Ben Saud and
"Raz."

Christopher Lampbert and "Diva."

Guru Maharaji
of India with
"Targa,"
"Beau" and
"Felicity."

Teri Copley
and "Smoke."

Index

All-Breed Dog Books From T.F.H.

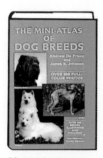

H-1106, 544 pp
Over 400 color photos

H-1091, 2 Vols., 912 pp
Over 1100 color photos

TS-175, 896 pp
Over 1300 color photos

The T.F.H. all-breed dog books are the most comprehensive and colorful of all dog books available. The most famous of these recent publications, *The Atlas of Dog Breeds of the World,* written by Dr. Bonnie Wilcox and Chris Walkowicz, is now available as a two-volume set. Now in its fourth edition, the *Atlas* remains one of the most sought-after gift books and reference works in the dog world.

A very successful spinoff of the *Atlas* is the *Mini-Atlas of Dog Breeds,* written by Andrew De Prisco and James B. Johnson. This compact but comprehensive book has been praised and recommended by most national dog publications for its utility and reader-friendliness. The true field guide for dog lovers.

Canine Lexicon by the authors of the *Mini-Atlas* is an up-to-date encyclopedic dictionary for the dog person. It is the most complete single volume on the dog ever published covering more breeds than any other book as well as other relevant topics, including health, showing, training, breeding, anatomy, veterinary terms, and much more. No dog book before has ever offered this many stunning color photographs of all breeds, dog sports, and topics (over 1300 in full color!).

More Dog Books from
t.f.h. T.F.H. Publications, Inc.

H-1016, 224 pp
135 photos

H-969, 224 pp
62 color photos

H-1061, 608 pp
Black/white photos

TS-101, 192 pp
Over 100 photos

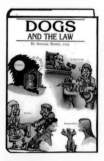

TS-130, 160 pp
50 color illustra.

TW-102, 256 pp
Over 200 color

TW-113, 256 pp
200 color photos

H-962, 255 pp
Nearly 100 photos

SK-044, 64 pp
Over 50 color
photos

KW-227, 96 pp
Nearly 100 color
photos

PS-872, 240 pp
178 color illustrations

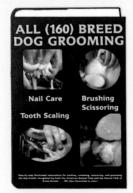

H-1095, 272 pp
Over 160 color illustrations

PS-607, 254 pp
136 Black/white photos